The Grand Literary Cafés of Europe

The Grand Literary Cafés of Europe

Noël Riley Fitch

Photographs by Andrew Midgley

NEW HOLLAND

Reprinted in 2007
First published in 2006 by New Holland Publishers (UK) Ltd
London • Cape Town • Sydney • Auckland

10 9 8 7 6 5 4 3

www.newhollandpublishers.com

Garfield House, 86–88 Edgware Road, London W2 2EA, United Kingdom

80 McKenzie Street, Cape Town 8001, South Africa

Unit 1, 66 Gibbes Street, Chatswood, NSW 2067, Australia

218 Lake Road, Northcote, Auckland, New Zealand

ISBN 978 1 84537 114 2

Publishing Manager: Jo Hemmings
Senior Editor: Kate Michell
Editor: Sarah Larter
Assistant Editor: Kate Parker
Designer & Cover Design: Alan Marshall
Production: Joan Woodroffe
Cartography: William Smuts
Index: Dorothy Frame

Reproduction by Pica Digital (Pte) Ltd, Singapore
Printed and bound in Singapore by Tien Wah Press, Pte Ltd

COVER AND PRELIMINARY PAGES

FRONT COVER: (top left to right) Café de la Paix, Grand Hotel, Paris; La Coupole inside and outside, Paris; Central Káveház, Budapest. (bottom) Brasserie Lipp (Paris)

SPINE: Giubbe Rosse (Florence)

BACK COVER: Café Els Quatre Gats (Barcelona), Caffè Quadri (Venice), Hotel Américain (Amsterdam)

FRONT FLAP: Cafe Odeon (Zurich)

HALF-TITLE PAGE: Les Deux Magots (1877), Paris

TITLE SPREAD: Café du Dôme (1897), Paris; Caffè Greco (1760), Rome

RIGHT: The backroom of Café Els Quatre Gats (Barcelona)

PAGES 6–7 (top left to right) Café du Dôme, Paris, Le Fouquet's, Paris; (bottom left to right) Café de la Paix (Paris), Literary Café (St. Petersburg), Caffè Florian (Venice), Giubbe Rosse (Florence), Café de Gijón (Madrid), and Café de Flore (Paris)

Contents

Café du Dôme, Paris

The Coffee-House Tradition

'All cares vanish as the coffee cup is raised to the lips,'
SHEIK ANSARI DJEZERI HANBALL ABDAL-KADIR (1597)

The coffee-house is like the wayside chapel that once restored religious pilgrims: coffee, the dark aromatic elixir of Arabica in a small white cup, resting on a round marble-top table; a bitter, irresistible taste on the tongue; and perhaps one's own reflection in the wall mirror. Simone de Beauvoir sits in solitude beside the glass in the Deux-Magots, sipping from the little white cup and recording her thoughts, the flow of coffee seemingly stimulating the flow of ink on the blank page.

In the café, the poetry of olfactory sensations restores memories of past delights, bright colours, and the play of life. The café becomes a pleasure dome, whether enjoyed at a table for one or enhanced with the additional stimulant of companionship.

The Science and Magic of Coffee, the Poetry of Cafés

When water vapour or steam is forced through the ground coffee powder and condenses into liquid espresso, air rises to the surface and creates a creamy froth. This steam caramelizes some of the sugar molecules in the coffee, which in turn form a network of bubbles, tiny air pockets containing the volatile aromatic molecules above the surface of the coffee. This foam of tiny bubbles renders the flavour both more fleeting and subtle, says chemist Pierre Laszlo. We cannot taste these aromatic volatiles in liquid coffee; we perceive the flavour only in the atmosphere above the coffee, when the elusive molecules drift up from the back of the mouth into the nose via the *arrière-bouche*. In order to be perceived, any fragrance – whether of coffee or perfume – must be volatile or vaporous enough to get into the air we breathe. We can distinguish between 2,000 and 4,000 different aromas, though those aromas dissipate rapidly. That is why perfume works best when sprayed as a mist; and why a really good espresso is topped with a froth or foam – what Italians call the *crema*.

The first sip must be taken immediately, when the volatile molecules are still encased in the minuscule bubbles, holding the flavour before bursting. Caffeine, the component that first and always makes of coffee a great magical elixir of creativity, is an odourless, bitter alkaloid also found in tea, cocoa and kola nuts. It can also be synthetically prepared from uric acid. Caffeine increases heart rate and affects the circulatory system, stimulating the bladder as well as the brain. Eleven billion pounds of coffee beans a year quicken untold numbers of heartbeats and charge the synapses with creative energy.

These are the scientific facts behind the vital concoction we call coffee: yet they hardly offer a full understanding of its power, much less the attraction of one's favourite coffee-house. The contextual setting and accessories of drinking coffee are vital – the marble table, the mirrors, a newspaper, or an attractive person at the next table: all these can cling like a bubble to one's coffee memory. American novelist Thomas Wolfe, enchanted by Paris cafés in his *Of Time and the River* (1935), emphasized the intangible force of what he called the 'obscene' intoxication of odours in a café: a combination of perfume, Gauloises, freshly roasted coffee beans, roasting chestnuts, cognac and espresso.

Not surprisingly, in France, Italy, Austria, Hungary, Switzerland, Spain and Portugal, it is almost mandatory that one taste the bitter sweetness of a coffee after the midday meal. This most ordinary yet extraordinary drink can round off any meal, its vaporous liquid finishing the sugar and salt aftertastes on the tongue, an afternoon ritual enhancing one's café dialogue or solitary contemplation.

The ancient world called coffee the 'wine of Apollo'. In Europe as elsewhere, it is the beverage of thought, dialectic and dream. Hence the union of coffee and the café in a symbiosis created to attract the writers and artists who have been sustained and nurtured by the establishments celebrated in this book.

Cafés are home to leisure, smoking, and conversation – staples for writers whose craft may none the less have been honed in solitude and privacy. They offer a clean, well-lit place away from a cold, dim city apartment, a dry haven in a rainstorm, a comfortable table at which to meet an old colleague. For the price of a cup of coffee, the writer has all he or she needs: drink, cigarettes, toilet, newspaper, telephone, heat and light, a table, a chair. The café is also a place for literary exchange with editors and publishers, a place for seeing and being seen, a place to read or gossip or debate, a place to start and end the day – being, by definition, open for long hours.

All these factors distinguish a café or coffee-house from a bar, bodega, restaurant or club. A café is more conversational than a tavern, more populist than a restaurant, and certainly more democratic than a club, which separates the classes and represents inequality. The café is devoted to leisurely consumption, its setting – at least, in those in the grand historical tradition – one of light, mirrors, windows and chandeliers. Its staple remains coffee. Coffee, and a sense of security, one might argue: a space where one is known and supported, conveying a sense of community that is both physical and psychological.

Cafés were more bourgeois than vulgar cabarets, more suitable for talk, good manners, erudition and society. Writers, philosophers, politicians, and liberal noblemen met and mingled in them. As Jonathan Swift said in 1722, 'coffee makes us severe, and grave, and philosophical'. Gradually the café became the descendant and precursor of the literary salon.

ABOVE: Marble-top tables and large windows illuminate Central Kávéház (1887) in Budapest, Hungary, frequented by writers like Zoltan Zelk and Friedrich Karinthy.

For centuries the cafés of Vienna, Prague, Paris and Florence have been central to urban cultural and artistic life. They remain today a mainstay of public life throughout the Latin and Mediterranean cultures. In the British Isles tea-drinking displaced the coffee culture when imports of the leaf flooded in from its Indian colony, and in colder climates such as Germany and the Baltic alcoholic beverages took precedence; yet here too, at the end of the 20th century, coffee experienced a great revival.

Stimulating Creativity: the Café as Workshop and Study

The writing and painting created in cafés have been recorded in countless memoirs and biographies. Arthur Symons wrote 'Absinthe Drinker' at the Deux-Magots in 1875. In 1898 Émile Zola wrote 'J'Accuse', his historic defence of Dreyfus, in the Café Durand (now gone), where the next morning his essay appeared in a paper mounted on a wooden bâton – as it did in 59 others in Paris. Kafka read aloud his first draft of 'The Metamorphosis' one Sunday morning in the back room of Prague's Café Stefan (now gone). Lenin and Trotsky drank and played chess at a back table of the Rotonde in Montparnasse. Federico Garcia Lorca met his friends at Café Gijón in Madrid.

BELOW: Leon Trotsky (1897-1940), a leader of the Bolshevik revolution in Russia, played chess in cafés in Vienna, Zurich, and Paris.

For many years in Paris, first in Café Guerbois and then in Café de la Nouvelle Athènes (both now gone), Manet, Degas, Renoir, along with, sometimes, Zola, Pissarro and Cezanne, gathered to talk. Sigmund Freud drank at Vienna's elegant Café Landtmann. Ernest Hemingway wrote 'Big Two-Hearted River' and rewrote part of *The Sun Also Rises* at the tables of Paris's Closerie des Lilas in the mid-1920s.

Many writers have given us vivid descriptions of writing in cafés. In a piece called 'Polyclinic', the German critic Walter Benjamin likened a writer sitting to work in a café to a surgeon in an operating theatre: 'The author lays his idea on a marble table of the café. Lengthy meditation, for he makes use of the time before the arrival of his glass, the lens through which he examines the patient. Then, with deliberation, he unpacks his instruments: fountain pens, pencil, the pipe.' Other drinkers become his observing students, and coffee 'puts the idea under chloroform'. With his pen, the artist makes his 'incisions, displaces internal accents, [and] cauterizes proliferations of words' until his words are 'finely stitched together with punctuations, and he pays the waiter, his assistant, in cash'.

On a cold, rainy day in 1922, American expatriate Ernest Hemingway leaves his apartment to find a warm place to write in a café on the place Saint-Michel. When the waiter brings his *café au lait*, Hemingway gets out his notebook and pencil and begins to write. 'I was writing about up in Michigan and since it was a wild, cold blowing day it was that sort of day in the story,' he recalls in *A Moveable Feast*. Because the boys in his story are drinking, he gets thirsty and orders a rum St James and continues his writing, 'feeling the good Martinique rum warm me all through my body and my spirit'. After a pretty girl 'with rain-freshened skin' comes in, he is excited and disturbed, sharpens his pencil shavings into the saucer, and begins writing at fever pitch, lost in the story. 'Then the story was finished and I was very tired. I read the last paragraph and then I looked up and looked for the girl and she had gone. I hope she's gone with a good man, I thought. But I left sad.'

The difference between the scientific German and the romantic American might be explained by their nationality or by the weather: Did Benjamin have clear sunlight for his operation? Did Hemingway's rainy gloom necessitate the lubrication of spirits and a female muse? These differences interest us less than the shared place of composition: the café, an environment for creative work.

The café, one close observer noted, offers a pause in the flow of time. The writer can keep an ironic distance from his own creative omniscience precisely because there is life going on around him and voices come and go. Indeed, the attraction of the café for the writer is that seeming tension between the intimate circle of privacy in a comfortable room, on the one hand, and the flow of (perhaps usable) information all around on the other.

The stimulation and nurturing provided by the café, and its central role in the intellectual and political development of European societies, lead naturally to a curiosity about the origins of the coffee seed and of the cafés germinated by its commercialization.

The Genesis of Coffee

Determining exactly when and where the coffee tree and its seeds were first cultivated is difficult at best because conflicting legends exist. Some believe that coffee was grown initially in Arabia near the Red Sea around the year AD 675. Most authorities state that coffee was 'discovered' between AD 575 and 850 in the province of Kaffa in Ethiopia, where the evergreen perennial shrub or small tree known as *Coffea arabica* probably originated. *Coffea arabica* produces a fragrant white flower that matures into a red fruit (sometimes called a cherry or berry) that contains two seeds (if only one seed develops inside the cherry it is called a peaberry). These seeds become the coffee beans. Some claim that as early as 580 Arab traders took the African beans to the southern tip of the Arabian peninsula, known now as Yemen, where the cultivation of coffee began some time prior to the 14th century (claims for the date of 575 are not compelling), and where coffee was used in the communal worship of the Sufi mystical orders.

The confusion concerning the origins of coffee is explained by the fact that coffee was not described in written records until the 10th century, when Avicenna of Bukhara, an Arabic physician

RIGHT: Branch of a coffee tree with fruits. Each cherry fruit contains two seeds, which are harvested, washed, dried and roasted. Each bean passes through at least 40 pairs of hands before the beverage is served.

Names for Coffee

bica (Portuguese espresso)
bunchum (early Arabic name)
bunn (Arabic for the two-part fruit or the beverage made from it)
cava (Slovakia)
joe (US slang)
java (US slang)
café (France)
caffè (Italy)
gahwa (Arabic name for coffee Arabica)
kaffe (Denmark)
kahvi (Finland)
kava (Portugal, Croatia, Czech Republic)
kávé (Hungary)
kahave water (early Persian name)
kahveh (Turkey; originally meant wine)
kofe (Russia)
kawa (Poland; pronounced 'kava')
mocha (Hungary)
turquerie (18th-century European word for coffee)

COFFEA *Arabica*

his monks the beans and was pleased to see that none of them went to sleep during evening prayers.

At first coffee was used as a food, not a drink. The beans were crushed and rolled into balls with animal fat to provide a source of quick energy during warfare and on long journeys, and to relieve labour pains in women: the first 'energy bar,' you might say.

Coffee was not made into a hot beverage until some time between 1000 and 1300, when its green, unroasted beans (the pits of the cherry) yielded a medicinal beverage somewhat like tea. It would later be used to make a fermented wine made from husks and pulps. Once made into a beverage, however, the raw coffee lost its high protein content.

The roasting of coffee beans did not begin until the late 14th or early 15th century, when the modern drink – made from beans roasted, crushed, and brewed with hot water – was developed. After the roasting and crushing and extraction process evolved, its stimulating effects changed the yield of caffeine and the popularity of the drink. The caffeine component of coffee fights fatigue and exhilarates by blocking the adenosine (a neurotransmitter) that slows us down or produces sleep. This effect can be used positively, for example in remedies for migraine, shock, pneumonia and poisoning. On the other hand, if taken in excess caffeine may cause irritability, depression, stomach acidity and insomnia.

The stimulating brew spread from Mecca and Medina to Cairo in the late 15th and early 16th centuries, and to Constantinople (Istanbul) by the mid-16th century. Turkish people claimed it was an aphrodisiac, and men kept their women supplied. However, it remained largely a novelty associated with Yemenites until the end of that century, when it became the universal drink of the Arabs (Islamic law forbidding the drinking of alcohol).

This was also the century in which news of coffee finally reached Europe, in written reports from travellers in Rome (1582), Venice (1585), Holland (1598) and England (1598). Before this, any writing about the brown liquid that prevented

BELOW: The Arabic coffee room of the Kaffeebaum (1695) in Leipzig, Germany. The multi-storied coffee-house also contains a Paris café, a Viennese café, and a museum.

and philosopher, praised the medicinal properties of what he called 'bunchum'. No references in Ethiopian literature appear before 1500.

As an ancient commodity, coffee has its own mythology, with several legends of origin conferring pious associations on the prized substance. The best-known has it that a monk or mullah (some say an Ethiopian goat-herd named Kaldi, who told the mullah) discovered that the coffee bean was a stimulant while observing a herd of goats chewing on the red berries of a nearby plant before running briskly across the hills. Apparently, he gave sleep had been in Arabic or Turkish. Historian Ralph S. Hattox gives us the best interpretation of these many early Turkish and Arab texts.

By around 1600 coffee had established itself along the caravan routes that brought trade goods to and from – and beyond – the Ottoman Empire, to what were to become the three centres of the Austro-Hungarian monarchy: Austria, Czechoslovakia and Hungary. Coffee was introduced into western Europe by Venetian traders in 1615 and Dutch traders in 1616, then spread rapidly across continental Europe during the 17th century – in large part because it was a strange and exotic drink (as, of course, were tea and chocolate). Coffee spread to the Netherlands in 1616 and to North America in 1668.

To the European traveller of the 16th and 17th centuries, Hattox says, the Near Eastern taste for coffee seemed 'bizarre'. However, in the last decades of the 17th century coffee became the beverage of choice for the enlightened and fashion-conscious among court and society. To drink tea, chocolate or coffee was to be a part of a larger and foreign world; to bring part of that world home and to make it your own was exotic and exhilarating. Having begun with the privileged, as a mark of wealth, fashion and cosmopolitanism, coffee-drinking eventually spread to the lower classes when it became inexpensive: in the 1670s and 1680s a cup of coffee cost a penny in London, one kreuzer in Vienna, two sous in Paris and one stuiver in Amsterdam, according to historian Ulla Heise. Only in Germany did coffee remain a luxury item throughout the 18th century, in part because the Germans consumed less and were critical of coffee mania.

Brews and Beans

From country to country, the preparation and taste of coffee differ. The basic process is broadly similar everywhere: the seeds of the lush coffee plant are dried, roasted, ground and infused with water. Heat acts upon the essential oils of the coffee bean to develop the aroma and flavour. Coffee beans can be roasted from light brown to a very dark, almost charred Italian roast. By 1885 the most popular method of roasting coffee was that using natural gas and hot air. Today, there is wide variety of both machines to make coffee and theories about making it, all aiming to preserve the aroma.

Whatever the method, the chief factors that vary the taste are the length and nature of the roasting, the freshness of the grind, the freshness of the water, the cleanliness of the utensils, and the absence of contaminating foreign elements. Adulterants include roasted and ground chicory, iris root, beans, rice, or the leaves of carrots, parsnips and cereals. The ritual preparation of coffee can be even more complicated than the pipe-smoker's ritual. A comparative tasting of ground coffee beans versus beans pulverized in a mortar, conducted by the renowned French 'gastronome' Brillat-Savarin (1755–1826), proved to him that pulverized beans made a superior brew.

One of the earlier descriptions of coffee-making comes down to us through the first major historian of coffee, William Ukers, who quotes a 17th-century professor at the University of Leyden: the Turks 'take of this fruit [i.e. the coffee bean] one

BELOW: Colourful bar and magnificent coffee machine in the tiled and ornate Catalan Café Els Quatre Gats, commonly called 4Gats, in Barcelona.

ABOVE: Many early coffee-houses use illustrations or carvings of Turks and/or a coffee tree, including this one in Leipzig's Kaffeebaum, to illustrate the Middle-Eastern origins of the drink.

Melitta Bentz, a German housewife, made a filter using blotting paper, through which boiling water was poured over the ground coffee, saturating the grounds gently. The coffee was then extracted below in a process taking from four to ten minutes.

Espresso, a version of coffee developed in Italy, is made by a process of extracting flavour from coffee beans by forcing water and steam through the coffee and into the cup. Luigi Bezzera filed a patent for a machine to do this in 1901; two or three years later Desiderio Pavoni, having purchased Bezzera's patent, began manufacturing the machines. Over the following decades many innovations refined the process and the result. M. Cremonisi developed a piston pump in 1938 that forced hot, not boiling, water through the coffee, eliminating the burnt taste caused by the Pavoni machine. In 1945 Achille Gaggia began commercial manufacture of the superior (high-pressure extraction) piston machine which formed a layer of foam or *crema* atop the coffee. The mechanism evolved from the early manual designs to those powered by an electric pump to a fully automatic machine that grinds the beans, froths the milk and delivers the coffee all at the touch of a button. Yet arguably Italy's greatest contribution to the coffee-drinking world came back in 1904, when Dr Ernest Illy developed the first modern, successful espresso machine, whose successors feed the morning frenzy in every Italian city.

Instant coffee, the bane of coffee aficionados, was first commercially processed in 1867 by the American Gail Borden of Illinois (though experiments had begun as early as 1838), and the first successful national brand of packaged roast ground coffee, called Ariosa, was put on the American market by John Arbuckle in 1873. Early in the 20th century Kedafa, a decaffeinated instant coffee made in Germany, was sold across the western world. In the middle of the century, after the Second World War, shortages of coffee saw the popularity of instant coffee rise markedly in the United States. Nescafé instant coffee, today the world's leading brand, was first produced in Brazil on the basis of technology developed by technicians in the Geneva-based Nestlé Company.

By the 1990s coffee and coffee establishments worldwide were seeing renewed growth. Beans received the same consideration devoted to grapes by oenophiles, with speciality coffees and

pound and a half, and roast them a little in the fire and then sieth [seethe, i.e. boil] them in twenty pounds of water until the half be consumed away'.

Turkish coffee is made from finely powdered coffee beans, heavily sweetened and drunk unfiltered by most Middle Eastern people. Westerners prefer clearer coffees. The French drink *café au lait*, coffee combined with scalded milk. Mocha, with its chocolate aftertaste, is from the Yemen region of Arabia, and other coffees are known by their place of origin: Sumatra, Java and Colombia. Throughout the Near and Middle East, coffee is both sugared and spiked with cardamom.

The world's first 'drip' coffee-maker was invented in 1908.

organically grown coffee beans attracting particular attention.

Generally speaking, two species of coffee are used for commercial purposes: Arabica and Robusta. The Arabian coffee tree (the original source) is classified as *Coffea arabica*. The Robusta tree is classified as *Coffea canephora* or Congo Coffee: a different species, native to the hotter and wetter forests of west Africa (and south-east Asia), and found today in, for example, canned ground coffee.

Coffee is one of the most labour-intensive food products. After approximately five years of growth, a young coffee tree bears the fruits of its first harvest. The coffee bean goes through more than 17 processing steps on the way to the cups of devotees. And the annual yield of a coffee tree is approximately one pound of roasted coffee! Or, to look at it in reverse, a pound of coffee contains roughly 2,000 beans and makes 40 cups of strong coffee.

Yet today, after petroleum, coffee is the second most valuable commodity of legal international trade. In dozens of countries coffee is the principal source of foreign exchange, and it is a major crop in 52 countries within 25 degrees of the equator. More than 20 million rural people work on coffee plantations though the world, according to Gregory Dicum's and Nina Luttinger's *The Coffee Book*, and every cup of coffee we drink is responsible for 1.4 square feet of coffee-cultivated land.

History of the Coffee-House

'The history of coffee-houses, ere the invention of clubs, was that of the manners, the morals, and the politics of a people.'
ISAAC D'ISRAELI, *CURIOSITIES OF LITERATURE* (1824)

The first coffee-houses opened in the early 16th century in the Ottoman Empire. In these special places, which sprang up in Mecca (1511) Cairo (1532) and Constantinople (1554), there were games of chess, discussions of news, singing and dancing. And coffee, it should be pointed out, was never the only drink served. Coffee-houses were known as 'schools of the cultured', an accolade echoed in the words of Sheikh Ansari Djezeri Hanball Abdal-Kadir:

ABOVE: Plucking the coffee-cherries. Each pound of coffee contains 4,000 beans, most of which are handpicked.

'Oh Coffee, you dispel the worries of the Great, you point the way to those who have wandered from the path of knowledge. Coffee is the drink of the friends of God, and of His servants who seek wisdom.'
(1587)

Because coffee was probably brought up through the port of Venice, many historians believe the first European coffee-house was established in Venice in about 1645. Others say it was in Marseilles between 1640 and 1644); still others say it was in The Hague in 1644. But if you consider Constantinople part of Europe, the date goes back by nearly a hundred years. The first

ABOVE: Paris's Le Procope, founded in 1686, became a centre for literature and politics and the model for a décor characterized by mirrored walls and bright lights.

Alexander Pope wrote about 'Mocha's happy tree' and gathered the gossip for his mock-heroic poem *The Rape of the Lock*. One historian dates the high-water mark of the coffee-houses in England between 1660 and 1730; another between 1652 and 1780. During these years says historian Ulla Heise, 'the whole of English literature [was] resident in the coffee-house'.

The earliest coffee-makers and café-owners in Europe were Greeks, Armenians, Turks, Lebanese, Egyptians, and Syrians – joined in due course by Europeans dressing in oriental finery and Turkish hats. A Greek opened the first coffee-house in London, a Syrian opened the first one (Goldene Schlange, 1714) in Prague; in Venice all the early cafés were founded by Armenians, and the first to endure in Paris was established by a Sicilian from Venice.

During the first century and a half (1650–1789) of the coffee-house in Europe, says Heise, these establishments 'lent major impetus to the evolution of the bourgeoisie' and its 'emancipation from the aristocracy and clergy'. And it was the Netherlands and England – both with their bourgeois revolutions behind them – that provided the backdrop for this social and cultural development.

The march of coffee and coffee-houses across Europe was not unimpeded. From 1500 until well into the 18th century resistance was motivated by several factors, including distrust of the alien in general or the Arab in particular, national trade and monetary considerations, hostility towards competition among innkeepers, distillers and vintners, and fear of political agitation (coffee-houses were seen as 'breeding grounds of unrest'). Indeed, the first brief ban was imposed in Mecca in 1511, when the ruler of the city feared for his own authority. Conversely, some opposition to the coffee-houses came from governments that believed they promoted 'indolence and idleness'. Though King Charles II's attempt to close the London coffee-houses mentioned both unrest and idleness, it had an economic basis as

recorded British coffee-house was in Oxford, opened in 1650 or 1652. Students and faculty patronized Jacob of the Angel, where their admission and a cup of coffee cost a penny. Pasqua Rosée (an Armenian or Greek) opened the first coffee-house in London in 1652. Many followed – by 1739 there were 551. Runners carried important news of the day from one coffee-house to another. During the 25 years of their growing popularity, these so-called 'penny universities' brought about a shortage of legally minted coins. Coffee-houses met the crisis by minting their own coins or tokens, using brass, copper, pewter or gilded leather – all stamped with their house name.

The coffee-house as a literary environment was most numerous in London, where it became a dominant force in the 17th- and 18th-century world of letters. Will's Coffee-House, for example, was known as a resort of wits and poets. Among those who gathered here were Samuel Johnson, Jonathan Swift, Joseph Addison, Richard Steele, Richard Brinsley Sheridan, playwrights William Congreve and William Wycherley, Oliver Goldsmith, Samuel Pepys and John Dryden. At Will's, well, for no excise tax was collected on imports. Gambling in coffee-houses also occasionally attracted negative publicity and censure. A final source of resistance in several countries was the medical profession, but these protests usually reflected pressure from government or other opponents.

The coffee-houses of the 17th, 18th, and 19th centuries were arenas in which the dramas of civic life were played out, from the separate cafés of the battling Whigs and Tories in 17th-century London to Paris's Le Procope and Café de Foy in the French Revolution. Coffee-house politics, which usually meant political opposition to the government of the day, was prominent in central Europe in the 19th century, where conspiracies were hatched in the coffee-houses, parlours and confectionery shops: the Red Room in Café Stehely in Berlin (where the Young Hegelians met), Vienna's Silbernes Kaffeehaus, Venice's Caffè Florian (where the anarchist Carbunari met his group), Padua's Caffè Pedrocchi (a battleground during the student rebellion of 1848) and Berlin's so-called 'coffee-tents' in the Zoological Gardens (Tiergarten). Twentieth-century examples include Paris cafés during the student rebellion of 1968 and Prague cafés in the Czech Velvet Revolution in 1989.

Cafés in the 19th and 20th Centuries

During the Belle Époque, the period that spanned the end of the 19th century and the beginning of the 20th century (approximately 1890 to 1914), literature and art took up residence in the coffee-houses. In contrast to earlier periods, when the artistic habitués of the cafés had deliberately set out to contribute to a middle-class culture by founding societies and newspapers, café artists were now against bourgeois literature and art. Many had been set adrift by political upheavals. They positioned themselves as a subculture of intellectuals, the bohemians.

The bohemian artists – the famous, the notorious and the insignificant alike – set up camp in coffee-houses, sometimes practically living there (the Symbolist poet Charles Baudelaire at the Café Riche in Paris and the Futurist writer Marinetti at the elegant Corso café in Rome are but two examples). At the other end of the spectrum of hospitality was the Russian Poets' Café in Moscow frequented by Ilya Ehrenburg, which was little more than a simple room with table and chair. When he emigrated to

Names for Cafés and Coffee-Houses

brasileira (Portugal)

café (France) (in The Netherlands: a bar)

Café-Konditorei (Germany, café-confectionery, as **Kafeekonditorei** in Austria, **konditori** in Denmark, and **konditeri** in Hungary)

caffè (Italy)

coffee-house (England)

coffeeshop (The Netherlands: a place that offers cannabis)

cafeteria or **cafe** (America)

kafé (Sweden)

kafe (Russia)

kafeneía (Greece)

Kaffeehaus (Germany, Austria)

kavárna (Czech Republic)

kávéház (Hungary)

kawiarnia (Poland)

koffiehuis (The Netherlands)

Konzertcafé (Austria: café with musical entertainment, as **café-concert** in France and Italy)

Paris, he gravitated to the Montparnasse cafés, also known as *les cafés de bohème* – particularly the Dôme, where many Germans also settled in. The Futurists and the Dadaists wrote their manifestos in cafés like the Voltaire in Zurich, where on 8 February 1916 Tristan Tzara and his band penned their anti-art declaration ('Vomited up from the slaughterhouse of the world war, we turned to art…'). Their use of junk and trash in modern artworks, as well as their exuberant espousal of revolt, were articulated and nurtured here and in Paris's Montparnasse cafés.

Émigrés have been vital in the history of cafés, ever since émigrés from the Middle East first introduced coffee to Europe and established the first cafés there. Over the succeeding centuries, as revolutions and repression have driven people from their homelands, coffee-houses have given the refugees succour and support. Karl Marx and Friedrich Engels met for the first time in Paris's Café de la Régence. An officer fleeing Poland in 1830–31 recalled being grabbed in the streets of Leipzig and dragged into coffee-houses to be treated like a god. A favourite of immigrants in Leipzig was a three-storey German coffee-house (the middle floor offered lodging) called the Coffee Tree. Heinrich Heine and Karl Marx fled to France, which offered them honorary pensions. Marx's German Workers' Association met in the Café des Boulevards in Brussels. Prague's Café Central was a bilingual meeting-place for the younger generation of both Germans and Czechs. Rainer Marie Rilke, who was unknown when he published his statement of love for the Czech city, found a home at the Central, as did Franz Kafka and Max Brod. Prague's Café Arco (like the Central, now gone) became the next favourite haunt of the Central regulars, including Kafka and Brod.

The café continues to serve the function that the forum or agora of Rome and Greece once did. In some cities, notes an Italian historian, the cafés were to a large degree factories of literature, inciters to art, and breeding places for new ideas. Major figures in the world of the arts, whether native or exile, have found their meeting places in the Café Royal in London, the Café Américain in Amsterdam, the Café Slavia in Prague, the Café Odéon in Zurich, or in Paris's Le Sélect, Café du Dôme, and Les Deux-Magots.

Traditional Types of Coffee-House

Historians seem to agree that a linear or chronological history of the café cannot be constructed. Instead of seeing a continuum in the development of the café, it is more useful to look at the various types of cafés, including the Viennese café, the Turkish café, the hotel or palace café, and the café-confectioner. Each of these types is characterized by its size, décor, lighting, seating, type of food and drink served, and cultural ambience.

The coffee-houses of the Middle East in the 16th and 17th centuries were simple: a wooden hut with rugs or carpet on the floor, an open tent, or a plain ground-level room with wooden benches. Coffee-houses may have come to represent the nursery of the creative and the avant-garde, but they began here to serve the peasants in the countryside and the crowded urban classes of the city. Coffee beans were cooked over a charcoal fire and pulverized for the customer, then brewed or boiled according to the country's custom. The old Turkish coffee-house, male-dominated, can be found today in rural Turkey, Syria, Afghanistan, Egypt and the rural Balkans (former Yugoslavia, Bulgaria, Albania). In Damascus, for example, across from the Umayyadid Mosque, there is still a coffee-house cum storyteller's haunt that has been a literary centre for a thousand years.

From the mid-17th century until well into the 18th, in Europe and as far as the Ottoman Empire extended, the first coffee establishments resembled these cafés of the Middle East – small dark rooms, mobile coffee stalls, or the 'coffee ambulances' at every market and fair. They were lit by candles, oil lamps

BELOW: A German Dada journal, *Merz* (1923-32) was edited by poet and designer Kurt Schwitters and nurtured, as many revolutionary movements, in the Romanisches Café.

and/or open fires. The owners of these early European cafés were foreigners, and the places were named accordingly: 'Armenian-style', 'Persian' or 'Greek'. Coffee was also served in the Italian *bottega*, French *taverne*, German *Wirtshaus* and Dutch *Schenke* – and the names slowly changed to feature the popular drink. For example, Will's Coffee-House in London was formerly an inn called The Rose. In The Hague in 1664, *Schenke* became *Caffee-schäncke*, while in Italy the *bottega* became *bottega da caffè*.

These early European cafés were dim establishments of dark wood, forested with nick-nacks hanging from the ceiling and walls – more like refurbished public houses in the Netherlands, Germany and Italy (where they were styled 'Venetian' – long, ground-floor rooms with wooden benches and tables). Those first establishments, according to the coffee historian William H. Ukers, were 'low, simple, unadorned, without windows, and only poorly illuminated by tremulous and uncertain lights'. Rome's Caffè Greco in the 18th century looked like this. In a well-known engraving of a Paris coffee-house of about 1700, hats hang on pegs on the wall and the men (no women) sit at long communal tables across which papers and writing tools are scattered. At an open fire, coffee-pots await under a hanging pot of boiling water.

The coffee-tent, pavilion or (in German) *Kaffeegarten* was another type of coffee establishment, one that harked back to the oriental origins of coffee. These tents or kiosks began in the 17th century and appear to imitate the feel of an eastern lounge. At fairs, on palace grounds and on grand boulevards, Turkish coffee pavilions were very popular. More than other types of cafés, these open-air establishments, obviously seasonal, were more frequently visited by women. One historian identifies 19th-century examples as Zaandvoort's Bodega Kiosk, the Café-Kiosk Tomaselli in Salzburg, and Berlin's tents in the Tiergarten. Vienna's Café Milani opened as a tent on the Burgbastei in 1789. Today's equivalent would be the stalls serving coffee in train stations or in the atriums of

ABOVE: Amsterdam's Café Américain (1882) is a beautiful example of the grand Art Nouveau style, with its decorated, sweeping arches and leaded windows. Later renovations brought in Art Deco touches.

shopping malls (called *Stehkaffee*, or 'standing coffee', in Austria).

The proletarian coffee-house, of which there is scant history except for the work of W. Scott Haine, was and remains a gathering place for the lower classes and is perhaps the most numerous of all types of café. Charles Dickens wrote about them in his novels, Friedrich Engels talked about the workers in these stalls or workers' cafés, and Gustave Doré's woodcarvings portray their wooden booths and low ceilings. Today these cafés still exist in the country for rural workers, in poor industrial areas of cities, at places frequented by lorry and taxi drivers.

ABOVE: Gustave Doré's engraving of a coffee-house in London's working-class district of Whitechapel illustrates the early dark and crowded proletarian cafés.

Padua, a sterling example of Italian neo-classicism. A few of these revivals still exist in resort areas, such as Monte Carlo's Café de Paris. The palatial Jockey Club (1865) on the Right Bank of the Seine included a public café, billiard hall, dining room, four gaming rooms and a sports hall. Those that have survived into the 21st century are characterized by heavy, brass-handled doors, marble-topped tables, threadbare upholstery, and a long menu of coffee-based drinks and chocolate confections peculiar to each country – in Austria, served with a glass of water on a metal tray.

Today they will be more fluorescent and formica than gas lamp and marble. They are dubbed *Kaffeklappen* in Berlin and *petits cafés* in Paris – where, since De Gaulle's time, the French government has severely cut down on their number in an attempt to curb workers' 'idleness'.

The coffee salon or grand café, multi-roomed and usually multi-storied, proliferated in the early 19th century, resulting in the opening up and brightening of many earlier and darker cafés. An earlier classic example of this type is Le Procope in Paris, with its wall mirrors and marble surfaces – all taken from a former bath-house by the Sicilian owner Procopio dei Coltelli in 1689. The décor was widely imitated, including his large wall mirrors, which other cafés soon realized made their establishments appear much larger, and appealed to customers' desire to see and be seen.

In Biedermeier Vienna, the literati gathered in Ignatz Neuner's Silbernes Kaffeehaus (1824–48). Here, all the equipment and decoration were real silver, from the tableware to the door-handles in the *Silberkammer*. Perhaps the grandest is Caffè Pedrocchi in

By the 19th century Vienna and Paris led Europe in the number and popularity of their cafés – hence the expressions 'Viennese café' and 'Parisian café', though there is little difference in appearance or style between the two. Café-restaurants became more numerous after the advent of the restaurant in France in the early 19th century. Precursors existed in the *Gast- und Kaffeehäuse* of Austria and Germany, where coffeehouses were permitted to serve food – a practice that reflected both the need for greater income and the continental blockade of coffee beans from 1811 to 1813. Because brasseries historically serve food at all hours, Paris's Brasserie Lipp and La Coupole represent the combination of café in the front and dining room beyond. London's Café Royal is another excellent example of the café-restaurant dating from the mid-19th century.

The café–confectioner or café–bakery is a particular type of European café that became popular in the mid-19th century in Germany (*Café-Konditorei*) and Austria (*Kaffeekonditorei*). Owners of these establishments sometimes began as bakers or pastry-makers who subsequently received permission to serve coffee. With gas lighting and mirrors, a few cafés and café-confectionaries became marvels of luxury and technical inventiveness. In the Café Mécanique in Paris, mocha was pumped up to the table-tops through hollowed-out legs and poured directly into coffee bowls. Amsterdam's Gekroond Coffyhuys contained a coffee fountain.

Hotel cafés are a creation of the wanderlust that seized the bourgeoisie in the 19th century. 'Tourism', a word one historian (Heise) claims was first used in 1811, led to the building of massive hotels in European cities. Each one included a café, usually with a street entrance for the general public. These hotel cafés ranged from the modest coffee-room/lounge in some English and German hotels to the grand café-restaurants of the Belle Époque. In keeping with the imperial style of these 'palaces' in the major cities, they were often called 'Central', 'Royal', 'Bristol', 'Victoria' or 'Continental' – and political events and wars sometimes forced name changes.

The grander the hotel, the grander the café. In the Hôtel des Trois Rois in Basel, the coffee terrace, where both Goethe and Napoleon drank coffee, overlooks the River Rhine. Berlin's Café Bauer was another example of the grand hotel café, where the pioneering use of 'applied electricity' was first demonstrated in their brilliant lighting in 1883. Among others that have survived are Amsterdam's Café Américain, Paris's Café de la Paix, Prague's Café Europa, Café de Paris in Nice's Hotel Negresco, and the Café Nádor in Pécs, Hungary. Café Nádor, indeed, is an imposing reminder of the extent of the Ottoman Empire, to which all of Europe is indebted for coffee – as is the equally imposing mosque opposite.

Of the many events that changed the nature of the café, it is worth dwelling on two in particular: the spread of electricity and the invention of the Thonet chair. Together with the marble-top table, introduced in the late 17th century by Procopio dei Coltelli in the Parisian café that bears his name, the Thonet bentwood chair eventually became a typical feature of café furniture right across Europe and the Americas. Probably it was Vienna's Daumsche Kaffeehaus in the mid-19th century that first used the smooth circle of wood as the chair's back (with another piece of round circled wood inside). Design number 4 of Michael Thonet's bentwood chairs has a wickerwork seat. When Adolf Loos designed his Café Museum in Vienna in 1899, he chose Thonet chairs because 'since the time of Aeschylus there has been nothing more classical'. By 1930 some 50 million Thonet

ABOVE: The Thonet bentwood chair, shown here today in Vienna's Café Griensteidl, was invented by Michael Thonet in 1849 in Vienna and rapidly became universally used in cafés.

chairs had been produced. Over time, the Thonet chair and other commonly adopted features of furnishing and décor spread to the places where cafés had originated: today, Istanbul's Café Pierre Loti uses Thonet chairs and marble-top tables, and Cairo's Café Fishawy features oval Parisian mirrors (only the oriental water pipes are redolent of the Middle East).

If the various types of café have become universal, the way people drink their coffee continues to highlight national differences. The French dip their croissants in their coffee, the Italians swallow it like fuel; the Russians take it short with a long vodka on the side, the Austrians take it with pastries and a glass of water on the side; the Germans take it with strudel, the Dutch with elegant chocolates; and urban Americans take it as a 'power drink' with low-fat milk and other nutrients.

ABOVE: A variety of newspapers in the reading room of Budapest's Café Central (Central Kávéház) gave early patrons a feeling of being in a library with coffee service (always accompanied by water).

All these types of cafés continue to exist. Even the old Turkish coffee-house persists in the most rural parts of eastern Europe. In the most general way, one can also identify national types: the Italian caffè-bar, the Parisian café-brasserie, the German *Kaffeekonditorei*, the Austrian *Kaffeehaus*, all of which share the same cultural coffee-house life. Alongside them are new types: the cannabis-cafés, cyber-cafés and Starbucks of today make it clear that the nature of the café continues to change in response to the complexity and pressure of modern life.

The Cultural Contribution of the Café

Though the romance of café-sitting may be as strong as ever in Vienna and Paris, the historical and cultural importance of the café has been under-appreciated. The twentieth-century Austrian writer Thomas Bernhard, a daily habitué of cafés, said, 'I attach the utmost importance to reading books and newspapers every morning, and in the course of my intellectual life I have specialized in reading English and French newspapers.' In addition to serving as a personal reading room and the laboratory of sociable conversation, the café has given birth to social and cultural movements, artistic and political revolutions.

Like a library but without the proscription on conversation, its unique atmosphere has promoted both literacy and sociability.

Some writers who use the coffee-table as a desk have sought obscure, out-of-the-way little cafés in which to work. Georges Bernanos, a leading figure in the literary *renouveau catholique*, claims he worked in such hidden establishments: 'For hours on end I crouch in dim cafés which I have deliberately sought out because it is completely impossible to remain in there for more than five minutes if one is not to perish from boredom.'

In the old-fashioned, multi-roomed cafés of the former Austro-Hungarian Empire, there is often a reading room. Café Central in Vienna, one historian says, was a kind of 'library with coffee service'. The café as reading room and clubhouse continues, sometimes still at a single table. English clubs and the Royal Society began thus. Budapest's Central Carambol Club met at the Café Elite. The Historical and Political Association was founded from meetings in a Zurich café in 1762. By the mid-19th century Germany had seen the birth of many organizations that moved out of the coffee-houses, including the Trade Association and the Chamber of Commerce. By 1863, every coffee-house in Leipzig housed at least one cultural or reading group. The Hegel Society met in Austria's Café Sperl beginning in 1885, and the Club of Seven (*Siebenerclub*) which began meeting there about 1895 created the so-called Viennese Secession. Examples are fewer today, but at the Café Sélect, Parisian writers still gather monthly at the back corner table to discuss their writing.

The café's function as conversational and social arena reminds us that invention is not just a creation of a single individual, but can also be a social act. Even in their seeming isolation, German critic Walter Benjamin had his attending waiter and Ernest Hemingway his muse. Cafés offer a pool of privacy, or, if one wishes, a group forum. The words of T. S. Eliot remind us that we, the writers of today, are part of the long ages of our civilization and have a 'simultaneous existence' with 'the whole of the literature of Europe from Homer'. We meet that tradition spiritually, if not physically, in a café.

In one's café, it might be said, the three major settings of society come together: the family, the workplace and the neighbourhood. Thus the café is what sociologists call a 'sub-structure of interaction', providing motivation and economic and emotional support. Stories abound of the impecunious writer sitting beside his pile of saucers and waiting for a friend to pass by and pay his tab, or of the painter who settles his debt with a painting. The importance of the café for the artist is well expressed by René Prévot in *Bohème* (1922): 'I believe it was the Irish writer George Moore – or was it Stendhal? – who in reply to the question how might art be best promoted, gave the remarkable answer: "Establish cafés!"'

The vitality of a city lies in its neighbourhoods, and the café is a centre of urban neighbourhood life. This sense of community is especially vital to the arts, as most vividly illustrated in the Spanish *tertulias* (social gatherings to discuss literature or philosophy) at Madrid's Café Pombo and Café Gijón. 'I have the sense of being part of a family [in my café],' said Simone de Beauvoir, who worked upstairs in the Café de Flore on Paris's Left Bank, writing and correcting proofs. One can hardly read a page of Beauvoir's multi-volume journal without coming across a reference to a café meeting. She claimed that during the Second World War, the café community protected her 'against depression'. Cafés certainly nurtured writers, which explains Boris Vian's assertion that 'If there had not been any cafés, there would have been no Jean-Paul Sartre.' A century earlier, Victor Hugo, who frequented the cafés Procope and Voltaire, wrote about their 'immense hospitality'. A few cafés have even been named after writers, including Paris's Café François Coppée and Trieste's Caffè Tommaseo, the latter named for the poet Niccolò Tommaseo.

Almost always, it is the owner who sets the mood of hospitality (though today it may be the *barista*). The status of café owners in mid- and late-19th-century Paris is suggested by a statistic published by historian W. Scott Haine: here, it seems, the café owner served as witness in almost one-quarter of civil wedding ceremonies. Indeed, the owner of the café is often the king of his café community – two examples are Leopold Hawelka in the Vienna café named after him, and Don 'Pepe' José de Brito at Madrid's Gijón.

ABOVE: Always a home for Madrid's intellectual elite, Café Gijon hosted poet Garciá Lorca, filmmaker Luis Buñuel, and artist Salvador Dalí at its black and white marble tables.

In some cities great literary figures stand out as the ultimate café personalities, either because they gathered various literary groups around them at one or more cafés or because they haunted cafés, wrote about them, helped set their tone. Among these dominant figures in the 1920s and 1930s were Ramón Gomez de la Serna in Madrid, Friedrich Karinthy in Budapest, and in Paris Peter and Léon-Paul Fargue.

Out of this café community, undoubtedly fuelled by the caffeine stimulus, came newspapers, magazines and new artistic movements – from the Encyclopedists to Impressionism to Existentialism. Indeed, the entire history of European liberal arts has been associated with coffee-houses. *Greguería*, Spanish literary paradox, came out of Café Pombo in Madrid. The birth

Literary Coffeeholics

'Oh Coffee! Thou art the object of desire to the scholar.'
(FROM THE ARABIC)

The French philosopher **Voltaire** reportedly drank 50 cups of coffee a day, but the amount of caffeine in 49 eight-ounce cups can be fatal to the average human.

Alexander **Pope**, whose mock-heroic poem *The Rape of the Lock* was inspired by English coffee-house gossip, found a cure for his intense headaches by inhaling the steam of coffee, what he called 'Mocha's happy tree'.

The composer Ludwig van **Beethoven** was obsessed with coffee, brewing each cup with precisely 60 beans, carefully counted, particularly when guests were present.

Italian poet Giacomo **Leopardi**, who frequented Caffè Pinto and the Gran Caffè in Naples, adored his coffee sweet, requiring no fewer than 12 spoonfuls of sugar per cup.

French novelist Honoré de **Balzac** ground his own blend every day, a mixture of Bourbon, Martinique, and mocha, which he bought at three different shops in Paris. Today's pre-blended coffees are often a combination of six to ten different beans.

Swedish dramatist August **Strindberg**, in a magazine interview in 1909, said, 'I get up at 7 am and . . . make my coffee (for no one can do it but me, it was the same with Balzac and Swedenborg). Bad coffee ruins the nervous system.'

Coffee-drinkers in **Finland** consume more coffee than do the citizens of any other country in the world (28 pounds annually for each citizen).

of German music criticism can in part be traced to Robert Schumann and his circle of *Davidsbündler* who met regularly in Leipzig's Kaffeebaum to discuss the lamentable state of music. One historian claims that 'there would probably have been no Vienna contribution to the literature of the *fin de siècle*, no advance on the part of Austria in world literary status, and no Viennese Secession' had it not been for the city's cafés. All these artistic and literary creations were to some extent first written in cafés. English essayist Joseph Addison visited Button's Coffee-House on Russell Street in London to sample public opinion for *The Spectator*, which originated in that coffee-house, and to solicit articles for his periodical. Richard Steele, who with Addison created the first journals highlighting the morals of the day, presented the contents of his *Tatler* (1709–11) in columns dedicated to coffee-houses. The third most prominent weekly journal of London in these years was *The Guardian*, which began as the house organ of Button's and best illustrates the interplay among the café, journalism and public opinion. Addison placed a sculpted lion's head he called 'Reader's Letter-box' in the café and responded to his correspondence in a weekly column called the 'Roaring of the Lion'.

Drawing on the influence and example of Addison's *Spectator*, the Italian Società del Caffè, which included among its members the economist Pietro Verri and the jurist and philosopher Cesare Beccaria, published *Il Caffè* from 1764 to 1766. This opposition paper ran up against strong Jesuit censorship, but led the way in the Italian Enlightenment. Johann Heinrich Füssli, also committed to the bourgeois Enlightenment, translated articles from *Il Caffè* in Zurich.

Not surprisingly, the coffee-house became the distributor of daily news. At the end of the 18th century and beginning of the 19th, particularly in Hamburg, Leipzig and Vienna, the customer had a variety of papers to read there. In Zurich's Café Odeon, a reader in 1913 could sit reading six editions a day of the *Neue Zürcher Zeitung*. In the cafés of Prague and Vienna, the perusal of the daily papers turned the café into a reading room. Ironically, in England the creation of the daily newspaper was to be a major factor in the decline of coffee-houses, for it became unnecessary to visit the café in order to keep abreast of news. Yet in cities where the tradition was strong, such as Paris and Vienna, purists are still devoted to reading any and all of the newspapers for as many hours as they have time.

In the 20th century, Ernest Hemingway said that café gossip 'anticipated the columnist as the daily substitute for immortality'. At the beginning of the 1920s, students founded the influential *Solaria* magazine in Caffè Giubbe Rosse in Florence. And the satirical German magazine *Simplicissimus* was founded in 1896 in Café Luitpold in Munich. Especially in countries centralized around a single city capital, such as Paris or London, key cafés have been the centres of influence. If Sartre sneezed, it has been said, the whole of France caught a cold; and few single cafés can match the sustained influence of the Caffè Greco, a Roman gathering place for 200 years.

In two periods in particular, the influence of coffee-house culture has gone beyond a single artistic movement or its influence on individual writers. On a much wider scale, says Ulla Heise, both the Age of Enlightenment in England and France and the European *fin de siècle* were embodied in the coffee-house.

Because cafés are 'verbal arenas', to use cultural historian Roger Shattuck's term, they have become salons of democracy, where revolutions – both artistic and political – have begun. As early as 1585, in his 'Prologue to a Comedy', Christopher Marlowe wrote the following:

ABOVE: Manager and patron exchange news of the day at the bar of the Giubbe Rosse (1881), chief meeting place of Italian Futurists in the first decade of the 20th century.

*'In a coffee-house just now among the rabble
I bluntly asked, which is the treason table?'*

A mid-18th-century French visitor to England, the Abbé Prévost, was impressed with English coffee-houses, 'where you have the right to read the papers for and against the government'; in his view this made them the 'seats of English liberty'.

The French Revolution (which finally brought women into café life in France) had its conception in the Café de Foy and Café de Chartres (now Le Grand Véfour) in the Palais Royal, and satirical ballads fuelled by the revolutionary spirit were sung in Paris's 'singing cafés' (the Café des Aveugles, located in the cellar of the Café Italien in the Palais Royal, was the first such *café chantant*).

One wit half-jokingly claimed that out of the boredom, caffeine and pomposity of Parisian cafés have come some great books and ideas, among them Cubism, Dada, Surrealism and Existentialism. Tristan Tzara, Hans Richter, Hans Arp and Emmy Hennings founded the Dada movement in Zurich's Café Voltaire; Sartre and his friends founded Existentialism in the Flore in Paris. The ebb and flow of artistic and political movements changed the clientele of various cafés. Coffee is a radical drink, it has been said, because its function is to make people think – and when they think, they become a danger to the status quo.

As institutions of entertainment, socialization, and education, coffee-houses gave birth to the first social clubs and other social institutions, such as England's Royal Society, considered to have begun in 1655 with the student gatherings of the Oxford Coffee Club, which met at Tillyard's in Oxford. Lloyd's of London evolved from a coffee-house serving merchants and seafarers, where sailing schedules and shipping needs were listed and underwriters sold insurance. Workers at this insurance company, one of the largest in the world today, are still called 'waiters'. It is said that the auction houses Sotheby's and Christie's began in sale-rooms attached to coffee-houses.

One incident at London's Grecian Coffee-House (today the

Devereau Court Hotel) will illustrate the importance of the coffee-house to empirical science, particularly around 1700 when scholarship began to become specialized and universal learning to decline. On this occasion Hans Sloane (founder of the British Museum's collections), Edmond Halley and Isaac Newton dissected a dolphin that had been caught in the Thames before an enthusiastic crowd of onlookers in the coffee-house. The cafés of 17th-century England and 18th-century Holland and France were fertile environments for such advancements in science, and in literature and politics, meeting an educational need fulfilled today by the university or academy.

Today's Cafés

The number of grand two- and three-storey cafés (such as Bewley's Coffee-House in Dublin) has declined in countries all over Europe in the last 60 years. Contributory factors include the affordability of restaurants, the prevalence of television, improved living quarters, home coffee machines, daily newspapers, and the installation in towns and cities of public

BELOW: Montparnasse artists meet in La Coupole about 1930.

telephones and public toilets. Economic pressures have also threatened cafés, which find it difficult to pay the rent on people who order water, linger over coffee for hours and read many newspapers. Café owners can hardly compete with the turnover of a fast-food chain.

Yet, though the size of cafés has diminished as the pace of life has increased, some grand old coffee-houses of Europe endure – among them, Rome's Greco, Venice's Florian, Madrid's Gijón, and Florence's Giubbe Rosse. They endure for those who find their neighbourhood there and for those who value leisure. They also endure because of their architectural merit and their historical and literary importance to city and country. Fouquets in Paris, Café A Brasileira in Lisbon, and Caffè Greco in Rome have been listed as protected national treasures in order to protect the cultural history of the city against the ambitions of new owners in search of greater profit. Paris probably has the largest number of well-known and vital literary cafés today. Changes made in the effort to continue to meet the needs of their patrons will affect some of the cherished traditions. But then, according to sociologist Ray Oldenburg, the survival of the spirit and vitality of a café depends 'upon its ability to meet present day needs and not those of a romanticized past'. So now we have the cyber-café, café-bar, jazz café, club café, chanson café, mocha bar, book café, comedy café and cannabis café.

Yet while the cafés of today are taking on new forms, the real or imagined experiences, memories and expectations of the past have made the cafés featured in this book repositories for the ideal of the artistic life, in all its conviviality and indulgence. Little wonder that the establishments described and pictured here continue to emanate a powerful mythological aura.

In an age when our exchanges are mediated by mobile phones and computers, to be able to sit down and talk with someone face to face is becoming an exotic pleasure, no longer an everyday banality. To that extent, cafés have become a place of magic, and their future rests assured.

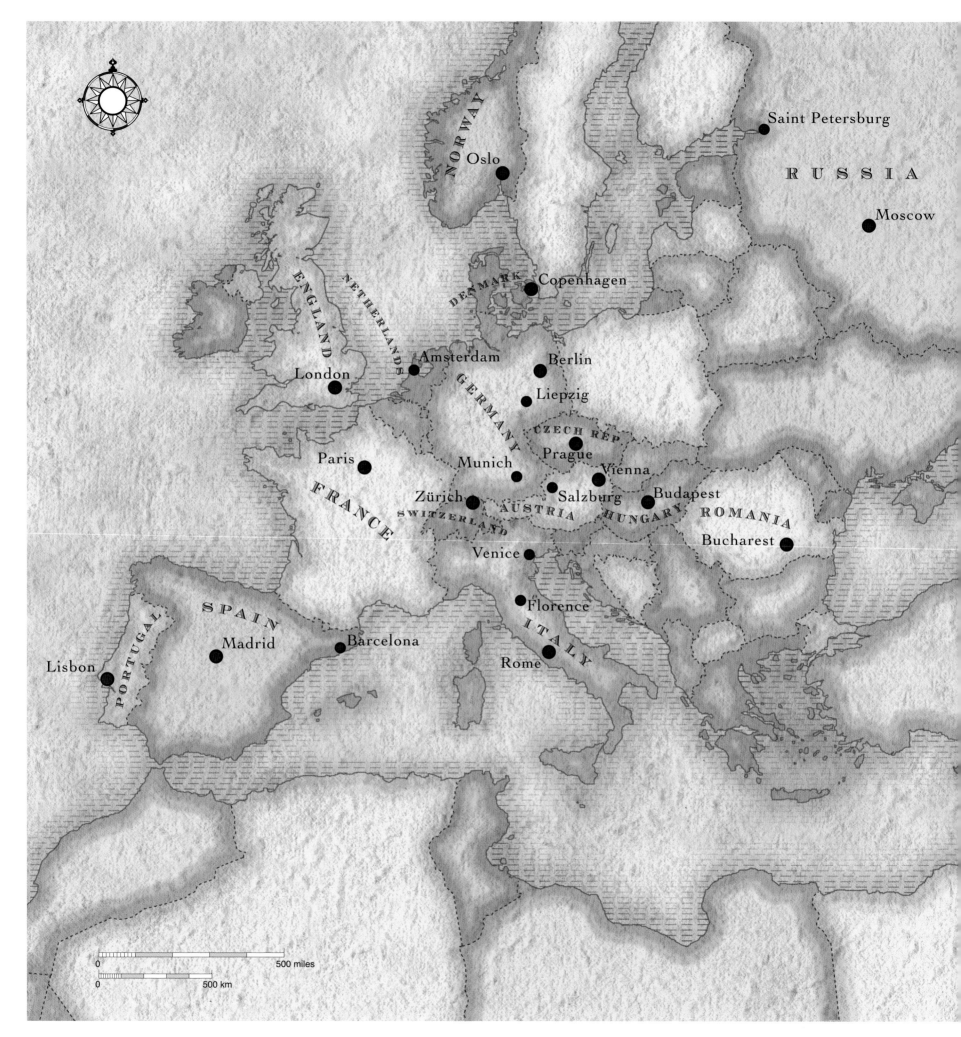

12 BOULEVARD DES CAPUCINES
PLACE DE L'OPÉRA, PARIS, FRANCE

During the rapid growth of Paris in the 18th and 19th centuries, cafés were built along the grand boulevards initially formed at the end of the 17th century when the city walls were torn down. The Café de la Paix is one of the few still open, in part thanks to its location in the Grand Hôtel and near the Opéra Garnier on place de l'Opéra. At the other end of the avenue de l'Opéra was the 18th-century Café de la Régence, where Napoleon once played chess, and just steps away were the cafés of the Palais-Royal, in particular the Café de Chartres (1784) – once the headquarters for the Revolution, now Le Grand Véfour, one of the most prestigious restaurants in Paris. The plaques above the seats commemorate illustrious diners, from Napoléon to Colette to Jean Cocteau.

Closer to the Café de la Paix, and along the boulevard des Italiens, were once the Café de Paris at no. 24, Tortoni's (no. 22), Maison Dorée (no. 20), Café Riche (no. 16) and Café Anglais (no. 13). Here was the heart of 19th-century Parisian café life – as illustrated in the fiction of its patrons Balzac, Flaubert, Maupassant and Henry James. In the Café Durand, Émile Zola wrote 'J'Accuse', his defence of Dreyfus, which appeared in print as a broadside in all the 59 cafés located between the Madeleine and place de la Republique.

The Café de la Paix, the last remaining grand boulevard café in this still vital centre of Paris, was built in 1872, the same year as the Paris Opéra. An example of the European grand hotel café, it is both a coffee-house and restaurant. The interiors are by Charles Garnier, also architect of the Opéra, and represent a celebrated example of the décor of the Belle Époque: *trompe-l'œil* ceilings of the sky and cherubs, gold highlights and marble pillars.

Nearly every famous international traveller, whether writer, musician, celebrity, princess or king, who has stayed in Paris has patronized this elegant Right Bank venue. A list of illustrious patrons would include Oscar Wilde, Caruso, André Gide, Paul Valéry and Ernest Hemingway – as well as all the opera-goers who congregated here on performance nights.

The best portraits of the café remain those to be found in the many works of fiction that use it as a setting, among them Zola's *Nana* and three characteristically American novels detailing expatriate experience: Henry James's *The American*, Thomas Wolfe's

LEFT AND OPPOSITE: One of the last remaining cafés of the Belle Époque in the Grand Hotel. When cafés lined the grand boulevards, the Café de la Paix hosted literary greats of the 19th century, such as Flaubert, Maupassant and James, who evoke the café in their fiction.

Of Time and the River and Hemingway's *The Sun Also Rises*.

After the rise of Hitler, the Café de la Paix became an important gathering place for German exiles. At the liberation of Paris after the Second World War, De Gaulle ate an omelette here before taking his triumphal walk down the Champs-Elysées from the Étoile to the place de la Concorde.

The café and restaurant, along with the Grand Hôtel above (where Henry James had his first private meeting with Ivan Turgenev), underwent major renovation in 2002–2003.

'And he would see them meeting every afternoon – that band of Bohemian immortality, that fortunate and favored company of art that could do no wrong – in some café on the boulevards, or in some quiet, gracious old place hallowed by their patronage, in that Latin Quarter, in Montparnasse, or on the Boul' St. Mich' or in Montmartre,'

THOMAS WOLFE, *OF TIME AND THE RIVER* (1935)

ABOVE: Irish author and wit Oscar Wilde was a friend of the leading French men of letters and of Café de la Paix even before he moved permanently to Paris in 1897, the decade of his greatest plays, including *The Important of Being Earnest* (1895). He died on the Left Bank in 1900 and is buried in Père Lachaise cemetery.

Balzac

Honoré de Balzac, who claimed he consumed coffee only when he was writing, best describes the electrifying effect of caffeine on the writer in his *Treatise on Modern Stimulants* (1852):

'This coffee falls into your stomach, and straightaway there is a general commotion. Ideas begin to move like the battalions of the Grand Army on the battlefield, and the battle takes place. Things remembered arrive in full gallop, ensign to the wind. The light cavalry of comparisons deliver a magnificent deploying charge, the artillery of logic hurry up with their train and ammunition, the shafts of wit start up like sharpshooters. Similes arise, the paper is covered with ink; for the struggle commences and is concluded with torrents of black water; just like a battle with power.'

For Balzac, caffeine is the power that drives the writer going to noiseless battle, marshalling his words and wit, in the act of writing in the self-created solitude of a café.

One of the legendary literary cafés of the Right Bank, Fouquet's has location, location, location – at the corner of the avenue George V and the Champs-Elysées, the most famous tree-lined boulevard in Paris, with its now newly widened pavements.

Fouquet's (the 't' is pronounced) dates from 1899. It began life as an Alsatian café and restaurant; the latter, Elysées

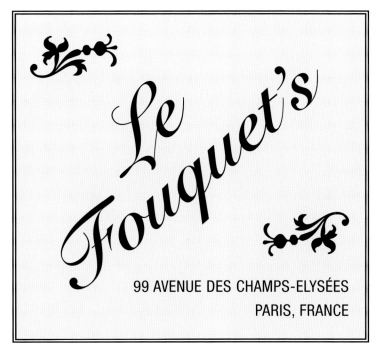

Le Fouquet's

99 AVENUE DES CHAMPS-ELYSÉES
PARIS, FRANCE

Restaurant, is upstairs today. Fouquet's drew the Irish novelist James Joyce as a regular in the 1930s when he was writing the novel that would be called *Finnegans Wake*: he would sip Alsatian wines all evening as his family ate. At one of these dinners with the Joyce family,

BELOW: Since 1899 the café to be seen in on Paris's grandest avenue has been Fouquet's. Though many tourists never get beyond the sidewalk tables, celebrities gather inside.

the Anglo-Irish dramatist Samuel Beckett met the American art patron Peggy Guggenheim, whom he escorted home for an intense marathon in bed – an affair she described in her memoirs.

Most of the famous patrons of Fouquet's today are members of café society and the French media. Though its appeal is to the international set of a certain age, the café is ageless. As the French writer Leon-Paul Fargue said in the 1930s, 'Le Fouquet's was one of those places that only go out of fashion in the wake of a bombing!' – a startling comment to read in the an age of terrorism.

The broad red awning sweeps around two sides of the building; inside, the décor is fake Rococo, with brass plaques bearing famous names that attract the tourists. The walls, too, are covered with pictures of famous patrons, including Marcel Pagnol, Marcel Achard, Steve Passeur and Henri Jeanson. The terraces on both sides are invariably full: that on the George V side is surrounded by bushes and preferred by the regulars, who today include film directors, actors and foreign journalists. Cultural historians like to add 'spies' to the clientèle, probably because of the international mix of people on the Champs. 'It has become a chic prize-ring,' wrote James Joyce in a letter to his daughter-in-law on 1 July 1934.

Fouquet's was designated a national treasure by the French cultural minister in 1988 to keep it from being closed when the rents were multiplied ninefold. The café is involved in the Roger Nimier literary award and the *Figaro* Magazine–Fouquet's Discovery Prize, awarded in a ceremony upstairs each year.

La Closerie des Lilas

171 BOULEVARD DU
MONTPARNASSE
PARIS, FRANCE

Once a carriage stop for noble travellers on their way south out of town during the French Revolution, La Closerie des Lilas has had a long and illustrious history. Named for the scores of white and purple lilac bushes that once grew around the café, in the 1840s it drew hundreds to its open-air dance hall. The café closed during the Second World War and reopened in 1953. Sitting where boulevard du Montparnasse meets boulevard St-Michel, La Closerie des Lilas is less than a kilometre from the expatriate café hub of La Coupole, Le Sélect and Le Dôme near the boulevard Raspail. Though it is still surrounded by trees, the only lilac visible today is in one colour of the neon sign.

BELOW: Founded in 1808, this 'Garden of Lilacs' was the meeting place of Symbolists, Dadists and Surrealists, as well as attracting the American expatriates.

ABOVE: French poet Paul Fort held weekly poetry recitals here before World War I. His name, as well as those of numerous other French writers and painters, adorn the Closerie des Lilas tables in the bar.

OPPOSITE: The dining area of the Closerie des Lilas has been added since its opening, and the menu has included quotations from some of its patrons, including Apollinaire and Hemingway. During the 1990s the menu featured Rumpsteak Hemingway.

La Closerie des Lilas now has a much smaller outdoor café, surrounded (if not guarded) by planted evergreen bushes. The interior contains a brasserie, a piano bar (with famous patrons' names inscribed on plaques on the tables) and a more formal restaurant. The lobster tank and grand piano have greeted regulars since the 1990s. This once bucolic watering hole has now become urbanized by the busy intersection and its noisy traffic, though the hedge of greenery provides some privacy.

The clientèle was diverse and illustrious. Ingres, Monet, Renoir, Sisley and Whistler were regular visitors in the 19th century. Other patrons included writers such as Chateaubriand, Balzac, Baudelaire and, later, August Strindberg, Oscar Wilde, Blaise Cendrars, Paul Valéry and André Gide. Among the musicians were Erik Satie, Toscanini and Gershwin.

The 'Prince of Poets' Paul Fort, who became a client in 1903, held Tuesday-night cenacles of prominent poets (it was called a school of poetry) which included Guillaume Apollinaire and André Salmon. Legend has it that Alfred Jarry, the author of *Ubu Roi*, once discharged a revolver (blanks, fortunately) into the mirror behind a lovely young woman, and then said to her: 'Maintenant que la glace est rompue, causons' (Now that the ice is broken, let's talk).

André Salmon recalls in his book *Montparnasse* that he felt honoured to have been invited by Paul Fort for an evening at the Closerie des Lilas: 'Fort went to no other café' and 'made of the Closerie the centre of the vast "Internationale" of the mind, poets and artists of all the world unite!' Among the painters and poets, anarchists and sculptors who gathered around Fort were poets Jean Moréas and the American expatriate Stuart Merrill.

Hemingway, who signed the *livre d'or* 'd'un client fidèle 1920–1956', writes about the café *in A Moveable Feast* and *The Sun Also Rises*. Here he would meet F. Scott Fitzgerald, Ford Madox Ford and Ezra Pound; and here he wrote his longest short story, 'The Big, Two-Hearted River'. He lived just around the corner, in the rue Notre-Dame-des-Champs which runs along the back of the café – as did Ford Madox Ford, Ezra Pound, Edna Saint Vincent Millay and (earlier) Whistler.

James Joyce spent an evening at the Closerie drinking with fellow Irishmen and proclaiming the superiority of the English language. Hemingway spent an afternoon with a friend discussing passages of the Old Testament, having found the title for *The Sun Also Rises* in Ecclesiastes.

Since the café's postwar reopening in 1953 it has become self-consciously literary, with all those brass plaques (though Hemingway's name is the only one on the bar) and literary quotations on the menu. Several brass plates on each little bar table bear names such as Valéry, Apollinaire, Chagall, Soutine and Degas – and Beckett, who would meet his editors at Seuil here until several years before his death.

The late French novelist Françoise Sagan, after writing 'Love Letter to Jean-Paul Sartre' in 1980, was invited by him to dine at La Closerie des Lilas. He was blind, and she remembers holding him by the hand to prevent his falling, and being 'so intimidated I could not speak without stammering'.

The coffee meetings on the terrace, the dinners downstairs, and the literary groups that gathered upstairs have all made this one of Europe's most important historical literary cafés.

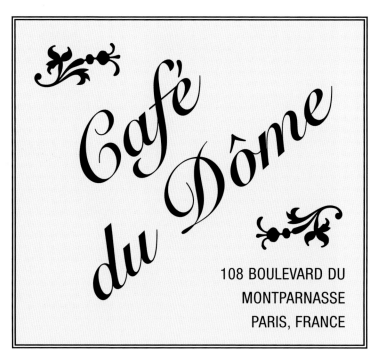

Café
du Dôme

108 BOULEVARD DU
MONTPARNASSE
PARIS, FRANCE

First opened in 1897 as a small working-men's café equipped with a billiard table, the Dôme later hosted the sculptors and painters who had studios in the 14th *arrondissement*. At the beginning of the 20th century the Dôme and the other cafés of the boulevard du Montparnasse became magnets for artists like Picasso who had left the hill of Montmartre in the north of the city for cheaper studios south of Montparnasse. It also attracted others from successive waves of immigrants, some fleeing pogroms, some just seeking the new in art; among them were Marc Chagall from Russia, Chaim Soutine from Lithuania and Amedeo Modigliani from Italy. Soon they were joined by political exiles such as Lenin and Trotsky.

Intellectuals once seen at the Romanisches Café in Berlin eventually showed up at the Dôme, some via the Café Central in Vienna. Guillaume Apollinaire, in an essay in *Mercure de France* just before the First World War, said, 'It is here that one decides which of the French painters will be admired in Germany.' Among the artists who drank their coffee or wine at the Dôme were Braque, Derain, Foujita, Kisling and Zadkine.

After 1920 the Café du Dôme became the most important meeting place in Paris for painters and sculptors, its significance heightened by an influx of expatriate American writers who helped to make it famous in the New World. The terrace tables spread across and along the pavement. Malcolm Cowley, who documented America's so-called 'lost generation' in 1920s Paris, claimed in a very American image that the Dôme was an 'over-the-table market that dealt in literary futures'. Individual careers were decided here, as they had been earlier at La Closerie des Lilas. By 1929, according to *The Paris Tribune*, there were 50 books in 15 languages in which the Café du Dôme was mentioned.

LEFT: The Dôme, which began as a humble café for French workmen and starving artists, became a hub for artists between the two world wars, particularly for emigrés from central Europe, including Soutine, Zadkine, and Chagall, whose pictures and commemorative plaques line the walls.

The History of Coffee in Paris

Coffee-drinking had caught on in Paris during the Turkish ambassador's stay at the court of Louis XIV in 1669, when Turkomania – with its porcelain cups, elegant coffee-pots, gold-embroidered napkins, floor cushions and exotic slaves – enchanted fashion-conscious Parisians. Molière satirized the trend in his play *Le Bourgeois Gentilhomme* (1670). Despite French physicians' warnings of the risks of illness and impotence, coffee's appeal became overwhelming and cafés multiplied. By 1716 there were already 300 in Paris, by 1789 approximately 900.

The Café de Foy was the setting for the beginning of the Revolution; Napoleon played chess at the Café de la Régence; Stéphane Mallarmé, Arthur Rimbaud, Paul Verlaine and Paul Gauguin gathered at the Café Voltaire across from the Odéon Theatre. The grand cafés of the 19th century sat along the boulevards – where Proust's Swann searches for Odette in one café after another – but by the second decade of the 20th century the centre of café life had shifted to the Left Bank, where it continues to thrive even today.

During the 1930s the Dôme hosted ever more exiles from the cafés of central Europe, as well as the young Samuel Beckett and the American novelist Henry Miller, an habitué of Montparnasse. Miller describes it in *Tropic of Cancer*: 'In the blue of an electric dawn . . . the Dôme looks like a shooting gallery that's been struck by a cyclone.'

By 1940 Jean-Paul Sartre and Simone de Beauvoir, philosophical partners and lovers, were complaining about there being too many Germans (some of the occupiers even brought their own tea and coffee) at the Dôme, and left for the cafés of the boulevard St-Germain, where the French artists regrouped.

Montparnasse saw a revival in the 1960s, but within 20 years the Dôme had changed its function to emphasize dining. Today the terrace is small and enclosed by glass; inside there is an upmarket seafood restaurant that few writers, invariably impoverished, can afford. Around the corner one finds Poissonnerie du Dôme, a splendid fish market, and across the street the Bistrot du Dôme. In the original building's restaurant, the Dôme's rich literary past is proudly displayed above the tables in dozens of framed photographs and plaques honouring past clients and the site's place in literary history.

'. . . you drank black coffee by choice, believing that Paris itself was sufficient alcohol.'

MALCOLM COWLEY, *EXILE'S RETURN: A LITERARY ODYSSEY OF THE 1920S*

LEFT: With a décor by Slavik, who designed the first Paris drugstores, the lights and windows are softened by peach-colored gauze, sheltering the neighborhood clientèle who read their papers or indulge in the favorite French sport of people-watching.

PREVIOUS PAGE: On the walls of the elegant seafood restaurant and bar inside are brass plaques and photographs of the painters and sculptors who frequented the Dôme when it was a workingman's café.

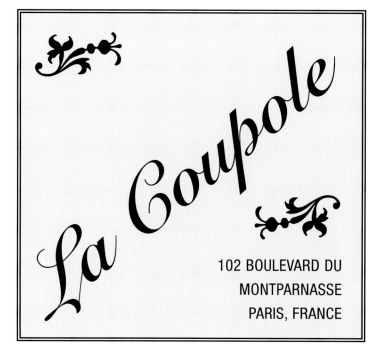

La Coupole

102 BOULEVARD DU
MONTPARNASSE
PARIS, FRANCE

Just a few steps west of the Dôme on the south side of the boulevard is the café–brasserie that became virtually the dining club of expatriate writers and artists between the two world wars. La Coupole opened at the end of 1927 in what was once a lumber and coal yard, and soon grew large enough to feed all the exiles haunting Montparnasse.

This 'sidewalk academy', as Leon-Paul Fargue called it, was a favourite of Russian émigrés, including Leon Trotsky and Igor Stravinsky, both before and after the Bolshevik Revolution. Here poets and painters learned 'bohemian life, scorn for the middle classes, humour and how to hold a glass'; and, in 1928, French communist poet Louis Aragon and

BELOW: This café and cavernous dining hall for foreign artists in Paris in the 1920s and 1930s still host locals and tourist groups for celebratory drinks or dinners.

ABOVE: The 33 pillars, each painted by an artist who lived nearby in the late 1920s, are historical landmarks that were preserved during the 1988 renovation. (La Coupole serves thousands of oysters a day—as well as a simple coffee to any newspaper reader or early riser. The ballroom is downstairs now, instead of on the roof.)

novelist Elsa Triolet met and launched the romance of the decade. Other regulars included Samuel Beckett, the French dramatist Antonin Artaud and the Latin American novelist Gabriel Garcia Marquez (*One Hundred Years of Solitude*). Lawrence Durrell, the English author of *The Alexandria Quartet*, admitted that he frequently got drunk at La Coupole, where from the terrace he 'saw all my heroes passing – I was young'. He called himself and his two friends, Henry Miller and Anaïs Nin, 'the three musketeers of La Coupole'. Françoise Sagan, aged 20 and writing *Bonjour, tristesse*, was a regular in 1954, as was the American novelist William Styron (*Sophie's Choice*) in the 1960s.

Beyond the terrace area, now enclosed by glass, is an enormous Art Deco-style dining area that seats 500. It is supported by 12 columns that were originally painted (to pay for their dinners) by students of Matisse, Léger and Friesz. Marie Vassallief painted the image of the black man in a top hat that La Coupole uses as its logo. Because they were registered as historical monuments, the columns were preserved and reinstalled when La Coupole was demolished and rebuilt in 1988. A high office building now rises above La Coupole, and the dance floor, formerly on the domed rooftop terrace that gave the two-storey building its name, is now in the basement. A picturesque fresh seafood bar is just inside the door to the restaurant. La Coupole serves several thousand oysters a day to a noisy and ever-changing crowd; but outside of mealtimes, a writer can usually find a quiet table in the bar, terrace or restaurant.

'*We sit very close in the café. We walk together very close. We are half sad, half joyous. It is warm. He smells my perfume. I look at his beautiful face. We desire each other.*'

ANAÏS NIN, *HENRY AND JUNE: FROM THE UNEXPURGATED DIARY OF ANAÏS NIN*

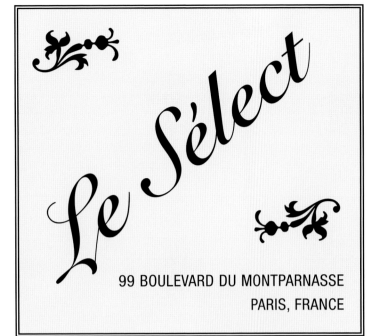

Le Sélect

99 BOULEVARD DU MONTPARNASSE
PARIS, FRANCE

Across the street from Le Dôme and La Coupole, at the corner of rue Vavin, is Le Sélect, which remains the least modernized of the three – a typical French café serving the neighbourhood. Joan Miró, Ernest Hemingway, and Simone de Beauvoir drank here before they became famous (Hemingway set several scenes here in *The Sun Also Rises*). Two notorious drinkers were regulars in the 1920s: English novelist Jean Rhys (*Quartet*) and American poet Hart Crane (*The Bridge*), who was once ejected, beaten and arrested for being drunk and not paying his bill. Barcelona painter Salvador Dalí swung his cape across his shoulder and swept in, unmistakable in his long curled moustache. Soutine and Pascin met each other at the Sélect and quarrelled after many whiskeys. Today, writers and artists still go to Le Sélect for coffee, private meetings and public readings.

Coffee-coloured walls, a green-and-white awning and a zinc bar are typical of the French café. Le Sélect opens out into the street in warm weather, but since La Coupole opposite was rebuilt into a high-rise structure it has lost its afternoon sun. Today, a cosy air-conditioned back alcove hosts meetings of literary groups; in the 1920s Russian refugees played chess there under the brick skylight.

The Sélect enjoys strong loyalty from its regular clientèle, who draw and write at the tables. After the Second World War

RIGHT: Since 1923 this café has quietly harboured artists, particularly painters. Its logo is an artist, with his portfolio under his arm, walking to Le Sélect. A new artist's work is hung on the walls each month.

ABOVE: With walls stained by tobacco, this is a café with a soul. Le Sélect has changed less than any other of the intellectual cafés of Paris. Artists and novelists still work at the same tables.

it became a favourite of African American writers, including James Baldwin and Chester Himes. Today it is popular with young avant-garde writers and artists, and has given birth to at least one literary journal. Neighbourhood regulars come at their preferred time every day, when they are not disturbed by tourists and loud noise. Noise is acceptable, however, on the days of special annual celebration, such as the summer solstice and New Year's Eve, when the Sélect 'family' gathers.

Now owned and operated by the third generation of the Plégat family, this is a café for the French. It does not seek publicity or sell its cups or other memorabilia for souvenirs.

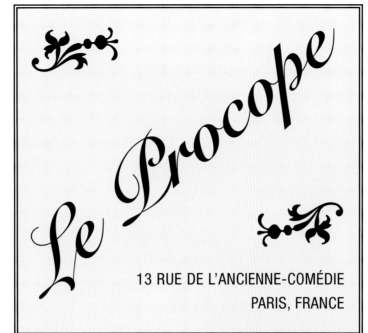

Le Procope

13 RUE DE L'ANCIENNE-COMÉDIE
PARIS, FRANCE

Credited with being the oldest (or the oldest still extant) café in Paris, Le Procope opened in 1686, during the reign of Louis XIV, when Francesco Procopio dei Coltelli, a Sicilian nobleman, imported sacks of coffee beans to Paris and opened the city's first large coffee-house under his own name. For two centuries, patronized by writers, philosophers and actors, Le Procope was a recognized centre of Parisian literary and intellectual life.

Procopio had had a coffee stall earlier (after learning his craft in the 1670s with Armenian immigrants Pascal and Maliban), but this new enterprise was altogether more ambitious. Its success was assured when the Comédie-Française moved in across the street three years after the café opened, and Molière and Racine became regulars. Later the street was named rue de l'Ancienne-Comédie.

An often overlooked feature of the Procope's place in café history is Procopio's purchase of a bath-house, whose fittings he had extracted and installed in his coffee-house: large wall mirrors, marble-topped tables, and many other features that have since become standard in cafés throughout Europe.

According to Alexandre Dumas, Madame de Sévigné fought against the consumption of coffee when it was introduced to Paris, predicting that cafés were a mere novelty that would quickly go out of fashion. But the Procope soon became both a vital literary institution and, in the 18th century, a political centre. During the French Enlightenment (1715–89) the *Encylopédie* was born here in conversations between Diderot and d'Alembert. Voltaire became the patron saint of the house (he was said to have drunk 40 cups of a coffee–chocolate blend each day at Procope), and a century later Balzac drank coffee here by the pint. Writers loved the free newspapers, writing paper and quill pens.

RIGHT: Le Procope was the birthplace of the 18th-century rationalist *Encyclopédie*, created during conversations between Diderot, d'Alembert, and Voltaire. The latter, perhaps the café's patron saint, met here with Rousseau and other giants of the French Enlightenment.

It was here in 1774, not far from the Odéon theatre, that Beaumarchais waited out his opening night of *The Marriage of Figaro* (it was a great success). Twenty years later Danton, an habitué who met here with Robespierre and Marat, was guillotined during the Terror (his statue stands defiantly nearby at the carrefour de l'Odéon). In 1790 the café was draped in black when its favourite American, Benjamin Franklin, died.

During the 19th century, when the number of Parisian cafés grew from 3,000 to 4,000, Procope's customers included Victor Hugo, Alfred de Musset, Théophile Gautier and Paul Verlaine – the last of whom held court at Voltaire's old table. In 1894, 200 leading men of letters voted Verlaine Prince of Poets at the Procope (his nearest rivals, with half the votes between them, were Mallarmé and Hérédia).

The Procope is no longer a centre for political and literary life, more a restaurant catering to tourists; nevertheless, one can still see the crystal chandeliers, gilt-framed mirrors and portraits of its celebrated customers, some of whom are listed on the plaques on the façade of the building. With imagination, it is possible to look byond the obviously fake 'period improvements' and imagine the café's glory days.

Three popular cafés at a major Left Bank intersection of streets, metro and bus lines – as well as the proximity of art galleries, publishing houses and authors' apartments – made the Saint-Germain-des-Prés quarter the crossroads of artistic life in Paris during the second half of the 20th century. However, it had had a literary character for a long time before this: the Flore opened in 1865, the Deux-Magots in 1875 and Brasserie Lipp five years later, and all three attracted patrons from the *fin de siècle* world of letters.

The Deux-Magots (originally called Aux Deux-Magots) takes its name from the two grotesque Chinese porcelain wise men (*magots*) mounted on pillars in the interior. Here Verlaine,

Rimbaud and Mallarmé, three of France's greatest poets, met, while the Anglo-Irish wit Oscar Wilde, exiled from England, walked here from L'Hôtel nearby to have his coffee every morning during the year before his death in 1900.

Visual art and literature have come into being at the tables of the Deux-Magots. Arthur Symons wrote 'The Absinthe Drinker' in 1875; Pablo Picasso and Georges Braque called the Cubist movement to life; Aragon, Breton and Soupault formulated their Surrealist Manifesto here with other Surrealists (Man Ray, Max Ernst and Joan Miró). Among the American habitués, Malcolm Cowley and his friends planned *Succession* magazine (1922–24); Djuna Barnes interviewed James Joyce (she was the only person who ever called him Jim); and Janet Flanner and Ernest Hemingway met in wartime uniform to talk about death and the suicides of their respective fathers.

The most celebrated period of this distinguished literary café's life was during the Nazi occupation and just after the Second World War, when French writers and artists moved from the Montparnasse cafés to the boulevard Saint-Germain to get away from the Germans. The Existentialist leaders Sartre and De Beauvoir made this café and the Flore famous, and the street crossing in front of it now bears their names. Today French intellectuals have more or less abandoned the Deux-Magots to the tourists, finding the Flore more fashionable; yet the Deux-Magots still advertises itself as 'Rendez-vous de l'élite intellectuelle'.

OPPOSITE: French Symbolist poet Paul Verlaine sits before a glass of absinthe, an emerald-green toxic liqueur distilled from wormwood and other aromatics which tastes like star anise. Outlawed in France in 1915, absinthe attacked the nervous system of Verlaine and his fellow poet Arthur Rimbaud (1854–91), who met regularly at Les Deux-Magots.

BELOW, LEFT & RIGHT: One of the best terrace viewing sites on the Left Bank, the Deux-Magots was the centre of French intellectual life in the years leading up to the Second World War. Inside, under the watchful eyes of the two wise Chinese men (*magots*), Sartre and Beauvoir wrote at their separate tables.

The interior of the Deux-Magots is a simulacrum of staid Art Deco, with seats of brown leather called moleskin (the Flore has red leather). But it is the crowded outdoor terrace, with its lines of tables and chairs facing the bustling Saint-Germain-des-Prés intersection and church, that draws the crowds, making the pavement a veritable social theatre.

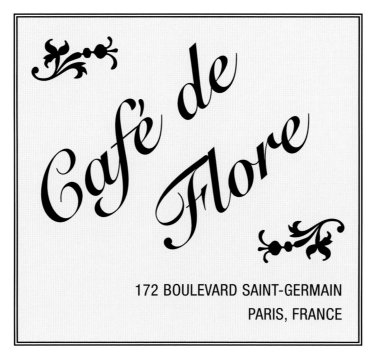

172 BOULEVARD SAINT-GERMAIN
PARIS, FRANCE

A corner neighbourhood café and favourite breakfast stop for many writers, editors and intellectuals, the Flore today is distinguished by a warm, homely interior and by its green-and-white awning facing the Brasserie Lipp across the boulevard. It was founded in 1865, here at the corner of the busy boulevard Saint-Germain and the narrow little rue Saint-Benoît. The name comes from the statue of the goddess of flowers and the mother of spring that at one time stood outside the café. Today the profusion of flower boxes in the summer continues to justify the name.

The Flore's past clientèle includes a veritable who's who of French literature and art. Rémy de Gourmont and Huysmans were patrons in the late 19th century. In the early 20th century Charles Maurras and his right-wing royalist group made the Flore their home, and Maurras used 'The Sign of the Flore' as the subtitle of his memoirs. Apollinaire and friends founded the magazine *Les Soirées de Paris* here.

Renovated in the Art Deco style between the world wars, the Flore was the café of choice after 1939 for André Breton, Léon-Paul Fargue, Pablo Picasso, Jean-Paul Sartre and Simone de Beauvoir (the royalists were gone by then). The two Existentialists found a workspace upstairs during air raid alerts, and in her memoirs De Beauvoir calls it 'our home': 'Even when the air-raid sirens sounded, we merely pretended to make our way down to the basement, but in fact crept back up to the first floor where we carried on with our work.' Thus it is the Flore, more than Les Deux-Magots, that became the unofficial headquarters of the Existentialist movement.

When Picasso moved his studio nearby in the late 1930s, he frequently met fellow artist Marc Chagall at the Flore in the evenings. Over political discussions, they doodled on napkins and matchbooks, often exchanging drawings at the end of the evening. Poet and screenwriter Jacques Prévert also scribbled on menus, toilet paper and paper napkins. After the war, when these satirical poems were published and he was approached too often at the café by readers and disciples, he decamped for the south of France.

Today's film-makers, publishers, and fashion designers have made this their regular haunt: 'all the cinema' meets here, says Daniel Gélin. Illustrious patrons of recent decades include Juliette Greco, Boris Vian, Jacques Lacan, Gianni Agnelli and Lauren Bacall.

OPPOSITE LEFT: Upstairs on the first floor is where writers could work quietly during the day. OPPOSITE RIGHT: The café's Second Empire style remains authentic and its tables crowded. 'Simone de Beauvoir and I more or less set up house in the Flore,' wrote Jean-Paul Sartre about their life during the Second World War.

ABOVE: The profusion of flowers reflects the name of this café, which was the establishment of choice for Huysmans and Remy de Gourmont in the late 19th century, L'Action Française in 1900, Apollinaire and Fargue in the early 20th century, Picasso and Chagall in the 1930s, Sartre and Beauvoir in the 1940s, and Jacques Prévert in the 1940s and 1950s.

Brasserie Lipp

151 BOULEVARD SAINT-GERMAIN
PARIS, FRANCE

Lipp's beginnings were as a 'brasserie,' meaning an outlet for a brewery where traditionally beer and Alsatian cuisine were served. Today, though the name remains, those items are only a small part of the menu in what is now a café–restaurant. With its painted ceilings, brass chandeliers, huge mirrors, and blue and yellow faïence tiles, what was once a 19th-century setting evolved into an Art Deco interior, and the building is now a designated historic monument. The distinctive tiles were made and installed by poet Léon-Paul Fargue's family business.

Léonard Lipp and his wife were among the many Alsatian refugees who migrated to Paris after their province had been annexed by Germany following the Franco-Prussian War of 1870. Initially they chose the name of a famous brewery in Strasbourg, the Brasserie des Bords du Rhin, changing the name to Lipp only after years of customers' insistence on calling it after the owners.

One of the most mouthwatering literary passages set at the Lipp can be found in Ernest Hemingway's Paris memoir, *A Moveable Feast*. He describes in loving detail the *cervelas* (a garlicky pork sausage sliced lengthwise and covered in a mustard sauce), served with potatoes marinated in olive oil and a *distingué* (a large stein of draught beer). As a warning to any of today's diet-obsessed American tourists who might come in while visiting Paris, the indoor menu clearly states: 'No salad as a meal.'

Jean Paulhan and the *Nouvelle Revue Française* group made this their headquarters in the early years of the 20th century. Fargue himself was a regular, as were Antoine de Saint-Exupéry, André Malraux, Albert Camus, Jean Genet, Alain Robbe-Grillet – and every French President, including Georges Pompidou, Valéry Giscard d'Estaing, François Mitterrand and Jacques Chirac. 'A great deal of intrigue and extracurricular government activity

OPPOSITE: Brasserie Lipp is a national monument with its beautiful mirrors, ceilings covered with buxom nudes, and Art Nouveau ceramic tiles designed and fired by the father and uncle of the French writer Léon-Paul Fargue. This is both a political café (every French President in recent history has been a client) as well as a centre for the creative types from nearby publishing and fashion houses.

LEFT: The bright, modern façade belies Lipp's historic, decorative interior and its now pricey fare.

ABOVE: Protective waiters still dress in black waistcoats and long white aprons, though the Alsatian brasserie dishes are now secondary to current favorites. One can still order dark beer, as did Ernest Hemingway and William Styron (*Sophie's Choice*, 1979), but fresh oysters and champagne are more common.

RIGHT: Spanish painter and sculptor Pablo Picasso had his studio (where he painted *Guernica*, one of his most famous paintings of the destruction of that Basque city) near Brasserie Lipp and the Deux-Magots.

used to take place chez Lipp,' wrote journalist Waverley Root. As Fargue claimed, 'One couldn't write thirty lines in a newspaper, paint a picture, or hold reasonable political views without spending at least one evening a week in Lipp's.'

Expatriate black American novelists Richard Wright and James Baldwin had a famous quarrel here. A decade later William Styron often dined with friends during the years he lived on the Île Saint-Louis. Writers who appeared on Bernard Pivot's long-lived television book interview show, *Apostrophe*, usually adjourned to the Brasserie Lipp with Pivot after their appearance. Today's loyalists and visiting film stars dine here for the tradition and celebrity more than for the food. Political guru Bernard-Henri Lévy presides as the Lipp's current intellectual fashion plate.

'The little cafés at five in the morning – their windows steamed over – boiling hot coffee.'

ALBERT CAMUS, *Notebooks 1935–1942*

Café Odeon

**LIMMATQUAI 2
ZURICH, SWITZERLAND**

The venerable Café Odeon stands near the northern shores of Lake Zurich, with the Alps as a distant back-drop. While Zurich was at one time one of the world's centres of finance with the fourth largest stock exchange, its elegant Café Odeon was the embodiment of the country's rich literary and political tradition of welcoming European radicals.

Going back to 1912, the building is structured with a high ceiling, marble columns, mirrored walls, comfortable upholstered red leather banquettes, steel-legged tables, lightweight chairs and a curved wooden bar with footrest. The style of décor is now distinctly Art Deco. In summer there are tables on the terrace. Though situated on a very busy thoroughfare, over the years Odeon has remained

BELOW: The classic Art Deco face of the Café Odeon, a haven for political exiles during two world wars and the Soviet reign in central Europe.

BELOW: Summer café patrons are sheltered by greenery and umbrellas while they catch up on the latest news and engage in convivial social conversation.

popular and trendy, though currently half the size of the original café.

Businessmen predominate in the morning; then come the literati and film-makers. At night the café is transformed by an exotic bohemian clientèle: nose rings, leather-clad men with hair dyed white, cool thin girls exuding a certain fake French chic.

This is the Swiss café most frequented by artists and writers, a place haunted by émigrés, political exiles fleeing persecution in the 18th, 19th and 20th centuries and finding refuge in Switzerland – among them Nietzsche, Trotsky, Mussolini, Mata Hari, Lenin. Exiled from Russia during the First World War, Lenin sipped his coffee here, reading the papers and dreaming of a Russian Revolution, while declaring: 'The neutrality of Switzerland is a bourgeois fraud and means submission to the imperialist war.' Ironically, when he triumphed in Russia, it was the deposed Russian aristocrats who replaced him at the café chairs.

Pacifists gathered in Switzerland, but specifically in Zurich cafés, during the First World War to draw up their manifestos. Café Odeon was their most popular haunt. Guests included Ludwig Rubiner, Yvan and Claire Goll, Hans and Sophie Arp, Hugo Ball, Tristan Tzara, Else Lasker-Schüler, Emil Ludwig, Albert Einstein and the peripatetic Austrian poet and novelist Stefan Zweig. Customers kept up with the political news by reading the *Neue Zürcher Zeitung* all day (but probably not all six daily issues of the paper).

The Swiss composer Ernest Bloch, having returned to Zurich from the US, met his acquaintances daily in the Café Odeon. Upon his expulsion from Switzerland in 1934, he bid them all farewell by declaring: 'A great tradition [of harboring exiles] could not have been more stupidly tarnished.' Two famous 20th-century exiles were the German novelist Thomas Mann, in Switzerland from 1933 until he fled to the US (returning in 1953), and Italian novelist Ignazio Silone, there from 1930 to

1945. Silone was being treated by Carl Jung, a student and then colleague of Freud, who had broken with his mentor's doctrine to found his own school. Called 'analytical psychology,' it was based upon the relation of the individual to what Jung called the 'collective unconscious'. All humans, he asserted, share an inborn unconscious life that is expressed through archetypal symbols in dreams, fantasies and myths. The Irish novelist James Joyce would later consult him.

James Joyce and Nora Barnacle had stayed in Zurich in 1904 when they fled Ireland's Roman Catholic oppression and Joyce's alcoholic father. They returned in 1915 to find a city 'crowded with refugees'. According to his biographer Richard Ellmann, 'The [Zurich] atmosphere of experimentation braced Joyce for *Ulysses*,' published in 1922 in Paris. He found literary groups in several cafés: 'In the Café Odéon, where Joyce frequently imbibed, Lenin was a constant customer, and on one occasion, it is said, they met.'

Joyce regularly returned to Zurich during the 1930s, often to consult doctors about his eye troubles and his daughter Lucia's schizophrenia. In December 1940 he was in Zurich again, this time as a refugee fleeing the German occupation of France during the Second World War. Soon after his arrival he fell sick, and on 13 January 1941 he died. He is buried in Fluntern Cemetery near the zoological gardens.

After his Los Angeles years in exile, pining away for his Café Central in Vienna, the poet Alfred Polgár finally moved to Zurich in the 1950s and settled into writing his essays at the Café Odeon. The ghosts of visiting writers, Joyce and Somerset Maugham, were with him there.

In the 1970s a regular patron was painter Marc Chagall, who at 83 was completing the five exquisite stained-glass windows in the ancient Fraumünster Church.

**ALTER MARKT 9
SALZBURG, AUSTRIA**

For 300 years there has been a coffee-house at this location at the Old Market on the riverbank. Mozart's father Leopold was a habitué. The earliest record noted that in 1700 two Italians (Caribuni and Forno) and a Frenchman (Jean Fontaine) applied for and obtained a permit for the serving of 'coffzee, rosolio, tea, aquavit and other alcholoic berages' [*sic*]. Thus, this café is properly considered the oldest and most famous of the classic Viennese coffee-houses in Salzburg. It was founded here, in what is now called Mozartplatz, perhaps as early as 1705. Some 50 years later the owner, Anton Staiger, who advertised himself as a 'royal coffee and chocolate-maker', commissioned a portrait of himself dressed in grand Turkish costume to add colour and drama to his establishment.

In the 19th century ownership passed to the family of the opera tenor Giuseppe Tomaselli, who bought the café for his progeny. When his son took over in 1852, he changed the name to Café Tomaselli. Even into the 20th century the café was presided over by another Tomaselli, Karl, and his sister Lisl Aigner.

In Austrian fashion, the café serves patisserie and the coffee is presented with a glass of water. Traditional also are the international papers available for customers. The curved windows and wicker-backed chairs put today's visitor into an atmosphere of earlier centuries. In the summer months tables are set up outside at the front and on the upper-floor balcony, blending into the warmth of the Old Market. In colder weather, patrons hang their coats on hooks mounted on the inside pillars.

It was the Tomaselli's upper floor that drew Thomas Bernhard, Salzburg's most committed literary café writer. He was prolific, producing 18 plays, 22 prose works, five books of poetry and 250 articles; to his credit, his work was satirical and condemned Austria's Nazi past and present. His will forbade any performance or publication of his work in Austria (which is why many people think he was German or Swiss). In a rant on cafés in *Wittgenstein's Uncle* (1986), Bernhard writes,

'I have always suffered from the Viennese coffeehouse disease. I have suffered more from this disease than from any other. I frankly have to admit that I still suffer from this disease, which has proved the most

intractable of all. The truth is that I have always hated the Viennese coffeehouse because in them I am always confronted with people like myself… [T]he more deeply I detest the literary coffeehouse of Vienna, the more strongly I feel compelled to frequent them.'

OPPOSITE: In the summer months the front of Café Tomaselli opens to the outdoors on both floors.

BELOW: The wall panelling, polished oak-block floor, cane-backed chairs, and coats hanging on the column hooks make this a cosy and typically Viennese café.

tubercular) and hoping not to be disturbed. He also had to read the English and French newspapers every day (Austrian newspapers were 'mass-circulation issues of unusable toilet paper'). He probably went more often to the Café Bazar on Schwarzstrasse in Old Town, another classic coffee-house, because it was near the Salzach and its terrace catches the breeze from the river. In the wintertime, the elegant interior with its high ceiling draws students and celebrities as well as intellectuals. The poet H. C. Artmann was a sometime patron. The Salzburg publishing house

Bernhard, who died too young at 58 years in 1989, was a daily patron of cafés here and in Vienna, always choosing the best air (he was

Residenz Verlag is located nearby, and the café is still a favourite of artists and professors from the nearby Mozarteum Academy of Music.

The Viennese Coffee House Tradition

Other cities may claim the first café, but there is little doubt that it was in Vienna that the coffee-house took on its most characteristic form. In Austria the coffee-house tradition has endured longest, changed the least, and been the most imitated in Europe.

The first Viennese coffee-house was established in 1672 or 1675, probably by Franz Georg Kolschitzky, who had lived in Turkey. He is credited with the habit of refining the brew by filtering out the grounds, sweetening it, and adding a dash of milk. Another claiming to be the first coffee-house in Vienna is the Frauenhuber, where Mozart once performed. The oldest

concert café is Konzertcafé Dommayer, in whose ballroom the kings of the waltz, Strauss father and son, used to play.

The birth of Vienna's coffee-house tradition and of the first coffee stalls is often associated with the Austro-Hungarian Empire's victory in the Second Turkish Siege (1683), though coffee was well known in the city before that event. The gilded cafés of the city are reminders of the glory of that triumph, set amid the splendour of the city's baroque architecture and spacious parks. Opening on to the street with large enclosed terraces, these elegant palaces are like the whipped cream characteristic of an Austrian coffee.

The Café Central, said poet Alfred Polgár, is 'a place where people want to be alone, but need company to do so'. Vienna's Central is distinguished from other literary cafés by its massive vaulted ceilings, which have something strangely ecclesiastical about them. The cigarette smoke can almost seem like the incense in a basilica, and the intent silent readers like early Christians in the catacombs. Depending on the time of day, the café might also resemble a Bedouin tent, a bourgeois dining room or the antechamber of a royal palace.

Small wonder, then, that generations of writers who have 'lived' at the Café Central have written about it. Several saw it as a library with coffee service. Another from an earlier era describes the pale faces, the occasional torrent of words from an agitated reader, and the waiters leaning against the columns like bored prison guards. Yet another notes the newspapers hanging like dried fruit in their wood frames. Joseph Roth, in *Zipper et son père*, set in the time of gas lights, describes its noises:

'When the fuel ran low, they weakened, flickered, and projected zigzagging shadows all around. Then a female server climbed on a chair and with the help of bellows breathed in new life. The flies buzzed, the playing cards crackled, the dominos clacked, the newspapers crumpled, the chess pieces fell on the board with a dry sound, the billiard balls rolled with a muted sound on the felt covered table; the glasses clinked, the spoons

RIGHT: Once a haunt of Leon Trotsky, the Café Central is in the very centre of Vienna. This so-called 'Ferstel Palace' was damaged during World War Two and restored between 1978 and 1986.

Café Central

PALAIS FERSTEL
HERRENGASSE 14
VIENNA, AUSTRIA

rang, the shoes squeaked, the voices whispered; the water dripped sentimentally from a distant faucet, a dreamlike faucet which never shut off completely; and the song of the lamps dominated it all.'

The Café Central was founded in 1906 next to the Austrian stock exchange and not far from the Imperial Palace (Hofburg), St Stephen's Cathedral and the State Opera. The young architect

ABOVE: Peter Altenberg, the Central's most beloved patron (now represented by this sculpture), wrote: 'Conversations… concerning personal ambition, vanity, delusions of grandeur, and "putting on airs", should not run more than three hours. Otherwise the perpetrator will have to stand a French champagne!'.

OPPOSITE: Under the arched and decorated Gothic ceilings, Sigmund Freud once met with his colleagues.

Freidell, Sigmund Freud (who came to play chess), Karl Kraus, Oskar Kokoschka, Anton Kuhs, Adolf Loos, Robert Musil, Alfred Polgár, Leon Trotsky (who also played chess here), Frank Wedekind, Stefan Zweig, and representatives of the Communist International, who eyed members of the opposing social-democratic workers' movement across the room.

One of the memorable coffee-house incidents, often recounted, took place in the Chess Room of the Central when, in 1917, the secretary of the Minister of Foreign Affairs Cazernin rushed in, exclaiming in agitation: 'Excellency, revolution has broken out in Russia!' Reacting dismissively, the Imperial Minister for Foreign Affairs said: 'Sure, sure, so who wants to make the revolution in Russia? Maybe Herr Trotsky of the Café Central!'

The most famous writer associated with the café is Peter Altenberg (1859–1919), a painted, life-size statue of whom sits at his regular table, just inside the door on the right. Altenberg, the 'Socrates of Vienna', was master of the house, which he made his own salon. He was a 'homeless' poet (his calling card listed the Central as his address), the personification of the eccentric and sandal-wearing bohemian writer.

After the First World War, the 'Mocha Symposium' met every Monday around Franz Blei and Erhard Buschbeck – though reportedly mocha was not the chief drink of the group. In 1943 the café was closed. It remained closed for 43 years, but in 1978 work began on its renovation and the Central was painstakingly restored and refitted for its reopening in the 1980s. One of the scenes in Daniel da Silva's 2004 novel, *A Death in Venice*, is set in the Café Central.

'You compose a poem which you cannot inflict on friends in the street? Go to the Coffee-house!'

PETER ALTENBERG

Heinrich von Ferstel, after a long trip through Italy, constructed the building between 1856 and 1860, using Venetian/Florentine *trecento* style (coffee-house historian Georges Lemaire describes it as somewhere between Gothic and Moorish). The glass-covered inner courtyard can give the visitor a feeling of being inside and outside simultaneously. The Ferstel Palace, as it was called, housed the Stock Exchange and National Library – and later, this grand café.

Straight away on opening, the café became the focal point of Europe's intellectual elite. It remained the meeting place for writers, intellectuals, and revolutionaries until the middle of the 20th century, and was always referred to as a 'writers' café.' Among the regulars were Hermann Broch, Egon

**MICHAELERPLATZ 2
VIENNA, AUSTRIA**

The Griensteidl occupies an exceptional place in Viennese history, for in the last decades of the 19th century it became the home of the Jung Wien ('Young Vienna') group, a literary movement dedicated to overthrowing the stuffy constraints of Neoclassicism. Heinrich Griensteidl opened his first café in 1844, later changing its name to his own. The wood panelling, wall

mirrors, and a ceiling curving up between pillars are typical of many Viennese cafés.

Café Griensteidl was known as a centre of political agitation, particularly during the revolution of 1848–9 – the first heyday of the Vienna café – when the nationalists met here to prepare the overthrow of the Habsburg dynasty. On one side sat Viktor Adler, the Marxist 'privy counsellor of the Revolution',

and on the other side of the room were Hermann Bahr and the Young Vienna group. Elsewhere in the café were the happy band of actors from the Burgtheater and their director Heinrich Laube, who had been a friend of Heinrich Heine. The theatre folk occasionally laughed at the earnestness of the political groups. Yet one day when a waiter was uncovered as a spy for the government, a serious riot was unleashed and the man was thrown out and beaten.

Other political events and movements have been played out in here, including violent scenes when Prussia was enlisting Austrian volunteers to conquer Denmark and again when Prussia declared war on France in 1870. Champions of the socialist workers' newspaper, Gustav von Struve and his disciples of the vegetarian diet, anarchists, and the occasional antisemite —all these, and more, stirred the waters of café life here.

Many years later, Stefan Zweig (1881–1942) described the intelligentsia's obsession with the smoky and electric atmosphere of the Griensteidl as a place accessible to all which was 'most suitable for finding out what is new'.

The posturing aesthetes of the Young Vienna movement – satirist Karl Kraus called them 'the most tender blooms of decadence' – included its leader Hermann Bahr, playwright Arthur Schnitzler, Hugo von Hofmannsthal (one of the founders of the Salzburg Festival and the most illustrious librettist for Richard Strauss), Felix Salten (who wrote the classic children's story *Bambi*), and Peter Altenberg.

When news came out in 1897 that the Griensteidl would have to close, Karl Kraus (1874–1936) wrote as its eulogy a

tragi-comic essay entitled 'Literature Destroyed'. When the café did close – it was demolished that very year – the literary crowd packed up and moved down the street to the Café Central, which then became the centre of artistic activity.

Almost a hundred years later, in the summer of 1990, a replica (reproduction) was built at the original location where there had been a bank, but today's Café Griensteidl does not have the original's literary connection or ambience. That it replaced a bank is an ironic reversal of what had happened to so many old Vienna coffee-houses in the 1950s and 1960s, when they were closed and replaced by culturally sterile financial institutions. However, the view of the Hofburg palace just outside the window is the same impressive sight as from the earlier café.

'But the coffeehouse is still the best place to keep up with all the news. To understand this, one must understand that the Viennese coffeehouse is an institution without parallel anywhere else in the world. As a matter of fact, it is a sort of democratic club, where the cost of admission is no more than the price of a cup of coffee.'

STEFAN ZWEIG, THE WORLD OF YESTERDAY

Café Landtmann

DR KARL-LUEGER-RING 4
VIENNA, AUSTRIA

Vienna, the ancient capital of the Habsburgs on the Danube, claims to have had the first coffee-houses in Europe, though England asserts a stronger claim. The oldest of the Vienna cafés is the Café Landtmann, founded by a coffeemaker named Franz Landtmann.

Since 1873 Café Landtmann has hosted the patrons and stage celebrities of the Burgtheater next door. Opposite Vienna University, in an impressive corner building, the Landtmann was the haunt of Sigmund Freud, the founder of psychoanalysis, who played his favourite card game of tarok here with academic friends. Legend has it that Freud sometimes even

BELOW: Vienna's oldest café's survival is ensured by its central location near the Burgtheatre and City Hall and its wide, covered terrace.

BELOW: The Landtmann's curved doorways and elegant décor have long drawn in artists and celebrities, from Sigmund Freud to Willy Brandt.

held sessions with patients here instead of in his office.

Painters, sculptors and architects were drawn to this café by its sophisticated décor and wood-panelled walls. Prominent guests included, through the years, theatrical producer–director Max Reinhardt, actress Marlene Dietrich and visiting politicians, including Willy Brandt, both before and after he became German Chancellor.

The interior rooms are a bit stuffy in warm weather, so all the guests vie for tables on the large covered terrace. In the small front room you will find reminders that this was the ladies' room – meaning that no cigars were allowed! The four wooden columns at the entrance were created by sculptor Hans Scheigner and illustrate famous scenes from the Burgtheater's repertoire. The café has a rather sedate appearance for today's visitor, with its panelling, booths and tables, long mirrors, chandeliers and table lamps. In the classical Austrian coffee-house tradition, there is music on Wednesday and Sunday afternoons.

Today the Landtmann remains the haunt of politicians (the café is across the street from City Hall), students from the university, and actors from the Burgtheater. These creative and intellectual patrons are watched over by affluent middle-class regulars – and all, in the comfort of the Landtmann, enjoy the café's legendary coffee cake, a marbled delicacy called Marmorgugelhupf.

ABOVE: A billiards room was, by 1800, a common attraction for European coffee-houses, and owners of billiard tables had to have a special permit. Vienna was the first city to introduce billiards and billiard rooms to cafés.

LEFT: Landtmann's well-dressed evening diners met under seductive chandeliers, lamps and bas reliefs, mingling with the neighbouring theatrical crowd.

Café Slavia

NÁRODNEÍ TRIDA 1/1012
PRAGUE, CZECH REPUBLIC

With its beautiful view of the Vltava river, the Hunger Wall on the opposite side, the Charles Bridge and the Prague Castle, the Kavárna Slavia (Café Slavia) is at the heart of Czech café culture. It was founded in 1884. Since then, from its ceiling-to-floor windows, Prague's citizens have seen state funerals, goose-stepping ranks of Nazis, the invading Soviet tanks crossing the bridge in 1968, and the marchers of the 'Velvet Revolution' who peacefully overthrew communism.

The Kavárna Slavia was the gathering place of Prague's German-language artists and writers, satirized by Rainer Maria Rilke (born in Prague) in 'King Bohush', one of his *Two Stories of Prague*

BELOW: This backlit Art Deco wall illuminates an alcove near the bar, where poets, politicians and filmmakers meet. A glass wall separates the reception from the stairwell.

Fortunately for us all, Brod ignored Kafka's wish, edited Kafka's writings, and wrote the first biography of his friend (1937).

The interior of the café dates from the 1930s when the old Jugendstil decorations were jettisoned in favour of a slick contemporary design. Viktor Oliva's *The Absinthe Drinker* replaced the old triptych of Mother Slavia on the wall. Absinthe, a psychedelic and addictive drink distilled from wormwood, was sold at the Slavia though it was banned in most countries. Prague playwright and novelist Karel Capek, who gave us the word 'robot' in his classic play *R.U.R.* (1921) was a regular patron.

The Slavia was a meeting place for Tvrdohlavi, 'The Stubborn Ones', pioneers of modern Czech art who exhibited their work together in the 1980s and 1990s.

The poet Jaroslav Seifert, a Nobel Prize-winner in 1984, wrote a poem entitled 'Café Slavia' celebrating cafés and the importance of Paris to Czech intellectuals. He begins the poem with the short visit of Guillaume Apollinaire to Prague in 1902, and speaks of honoring Absinthe. Looking from the window at the River Vltava enables him to see 'the Seine under the dock flowing'. The Slavia has also given its name to paintings and novels. American poet James Ragan's 'Crossing the Charles Bridge' (1995) celebrates 'Seifert on the tram to Slavie', Kafka 'sipping absinthe with Apollinaire' and 'Havel with the sword of Bruncvik'.

Here at the Slavia, the film and theatrical community of artists gathered, including filmmakers such as Miloš Forman, Ivan Passer, Jiři Menzel (*Closely Watched Trains*), Jurai Jakubitsko, Jaromila Jireš, Vera Chytilova and Jan Kadar – as part of the Czech New Wave in the 1950s and 1960s.

Havel and others met here to plan the ousting of the communists. Ironically, the privatization of property that followed their 1989 victory saw the Slavia closed in a real-estate squabble. When, three

ABOVE: This grand building houses the Café Slavia, which is across from the National Theatre on Vitezna Street. The café attracted German-speaking Prague writers such as Rilke and Kafka.

(1899). Rilke changed the name of the café, but its identity is unmistakable.

Here Kafka held heated philosophical discussions with Max Brod in the fall of 1911, when Kafka awakened to the East European Jewish culture so denigrated by his German-oriented co-religionists. Brod was a Prague-born Jewish writer and composer whom Kafka left in charge of his papers with explicit instructions to burn them.

ABOVE: The Slavia stretches along the first floor and looks out at the National Theatre and the River Vltava (also called the Moldau). From these windows most of the Czech Republic's 20th-century historical events have been witnessed.

years after its sale to a Boston firm, it had not been renovated, a sit-in group that included Havel demanded it be reopened. The Czech Republic voided the sale to the American speculators and the building was taken over by Prague School of the Performing Arts (FAMU), which for a short time ran it on donations.

The Slavia reopened in 1997, restored to its 1930s glory, in what President Václav Hável called 'a small victory over stupidity'. From his hospital bed he expressed his wish that the café should once again become a crossroads of Prague's intellectual life.

Amid the Gothic splendour of Prague, now cleansed of Soviet cement-block sterility, there is a café still simply and shabbily redolent of days gone by. The Montmartre grew out of a working-class pub in 1911, and soon became the venue for Czech, German and Yiddish-language writers – the core of creative artists who nourished the strong intellectual life and coffee-house tradition in Prague.

Montmartre

RETEZOVÁ 7
PRAGUE, CZECH REPUBLIC

Down a paint-chipped alley is the dark green door leading into Café Montmartre. The interior, created by the Prague avant-garde architect Jiří Kreoha (1893–1974), has a typical early coffee-house décor with old wooden floors and benches, antique chairs, wooden tables of varying shapes, a chandelier emitting a yellow light, and a back room with armoires and more antique furniture. The Montmartre serves primarily coffee and apple strudel, standing proud as a café with no restaurant and a separate bar for spirits. Vratislav Hugo Brunner painted the ceiling, vaulted and low in floral designs of yellow and red. The beautiful piano is stained black.

In the centre of the café is a long, wooden and brass-adorned bar, whose regulars included reporter Egon Erwin Kisch, the multi-talented Emil Arthur Longen (painter, playwright, theatre director), Eduard Bass, and the Prague German journalist Arne Laurin, founder of the Prague Press. German-born Paul Wiegler created a monument to the Prague of 1910 in his novel *The House on the Moldau* (1934), including a full description of this café in chapter 4. He also edited the German newspaper *Bohemia* in the office block across the street, and later wrote books about Beethoven, Goethe and Schopenhauer.

Other patrons have included Franz Kafka, Max Brod, Jaroslav Hašek (author of *The Good Soldier Schweik*), Frantisek Langer, Frantisek Tichý, and the Prague-born Austrian writer Franz Werfel (*Song of Bernadette*). The names of Montmartre's most famous patrons are inscribed on the door of the café. Many of them also frequently patronized the Kavárna Slavia.

Even today artists continue to love the dark, authentic café Montmartre as much as their predecessors of a century ago, for it has become a key part of the rich cultural life of the city.

Frequently a venue for book fairs and after-hours literary gatherings, the Montmartre also hosts parties for literary works. On the ground floor is a collection of photographs and documents about the artistic patrons of the first half of the 20th century. Of all the historical cafés in now fashionable Prague, only the Montmartre has not gentrified its décor.

ABOVE: The Montmartre is a quiet place for reading and smoking until the arrival of the afternoon and evening regulars, which have included Prague's leading writers, Kafka, Kisch, Weigler and Hável.

OPPOSITE: Down a narrow street in Prague, the Montmartre is one of the most lively and authentic artist and student hang-outs, still as lively today as it was in the early 20th century.

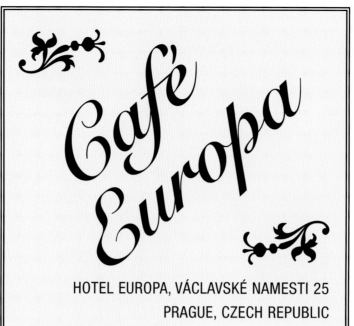

Café Europa

HOTEL EUROPA, VÁCLAVSKÉ NAMESTI 25
PRAGUE, CZECH REPUBLIC

In stark contrast to the Café Montmartre is the hotel café called Café Europa on Wenceslas Square. Founded in 1889, the café of the Grand Hotel Europa is the most photographed in Prague, full of Old World elegance. The building was initially called 'Archduke Stephan' and was designed by architect Franta Bêlský, but redesigned in the Art Nouveau style in 1903–1905. A balcony wraps around the dining room with its murals by Malers Peyda and its marble columns. The late-afternoon piano and violin music, along with the elegant wall-coverings, palm fronds and a grand skylight, give this café-concert a faded Old World elegance rare in the now touristy Wenceslas Square. Grand chandeliers, wall sconces, a tea cellar, and a bar with Far Eastern sculpture and bamboo complete the atmosphere of a grand hotel café on a scale rivalling Paris's Café de la Paix.

Café Europa, less boisterous and crowded than the other Prague cafés, has hosted many a writer who wanted a quiet writing table. The café is famous for hosting Franz Kafka, Max Brod, Franz Werfel and Jaroslav Hašek. More recently, film-maker Miloš Forman and novelist Milan Kundera (*The Unbearable Lightness of Being*) were occasional visitors.

Today Café Europa is occasionally deserted (except for the terrace) during the day, when patrons are more than likely to frequent the Louvre Café, once the choice of Freud, Einstein and playwright Karel Capek. The Louvre (at Narodni 20) opened in 1902, and it, like Kavárna Slavia, has been renovated.

ABOVE: This beautiful Art Nouveau (or Jugendstil) café, with its curving lamps and elegant mirrors, was created during the complete renovation of the hotel between 1903 and 1905.

OPPOSITE: Hotel Europa, dating from 1889, is the most beautiful building on Wenceslas Square, and its café offers a quiet haven for daytime writers even today.

Prague's Other Cafés

It was said in the last century that 'some Czechs judge a man's politics by the Kavárna he frequents and the papers he reads', but it would seem that the writers in Prague have chosen a number of cafés depending upon the time of day and their own needs.

Among the distinguished cafés of old Prague that are now gone were Café Arco (Kafka, Brod, Franz Werfel, and Egon Erwin Kisch); Café Central (Rainer Maria Rilke, Kafka, Kisch); Café Savoy (Werfel); and Café Continental (German Jewish intelligentsia including Julius Fucik, Kisch, Willi Bredel, Hans Beimler and Johannes R. Becher), once housed in Slovansky Dúm.

Enduring cafés such as the Europa (joined now by several new cafés) maintain the great Prague coffee-house tradition. During the last 15 years, expatriate writers (including this author) have given readings at the Globe Bookstore Café. In the vegetarian FX Café in the Radost building, Havel had drinks with playwrights Arthur Miller, Edward Albee, Tom Stoppard and Ronald Harwood after an evening meeting of the International PEN in 1994.

Café
Gerbeaud

VÖRÖSMARTY TÉR 7
BUDAPEST, HUNGARY

The two cities of Buda (and Óbuda) and Pest, divided by the Danube river, have a long coffee-house tradition. At one time more than 500 coffee-houses thrived, modelled on those in Vienna and Paris. Today it is on the Pest side of the river that the cafés are to be found.

Hungary's coffee is influenced by the Turkish tradition: boiled and unfiltered, served very strong, straight and heavily sugared. Recently, thanks to the influence of west European countries, Hungarians have begun drinking, and brewing, milder and more refined coffee to suit other tastes.

In 1884 Émile Gerbeaud, a Geneva capitalist, opened a shop here and made it into one of Europe's leading social meeting places. He also made himself the emperor of the Hungarian

pastry industry and is reputed to have created the chocolate-covered cherry. The Gerbeaud name has been synonymous with fine Hungarian chocolate ever since. The café is still considered to have an excellent pastry selection, its speciality, the Gerbeaud slice, consisting of layers of sweet dough layered with jam and nuts and iced with chocolate.

Some call Gerbeaud the 'queen' of the city's cafés, for its beauty and because it was one of the most important rendezvous for the literati of Old Hungary at a time when Budapest's cafés were among the best in the Austro-Hungarian Empire. Each artistic movement from Symbolism through to Modernism was reported in the chronicles written here and in the Kávéház New York and Central Kávéház.

A restrained elegance radiates peace and quiet here in rooms illuminated by chandeliers and crystal ceiling lamps. The café is dominated by a counter 10 metres long, carved and marble-topped, on which elegant cakes are arranged on glass shelves. This grand display of a classical *café-konditeri* attracts pastry devotees. The long list of coffees is in the great Austro-Hungarian tradition.

During the Nazi and the communist eras, and because Gerbeaud had been a Swiss capitalist, the café was renamed Vörösmarty Cukrászda, after the nation's best-loved 19th-century nationalist poet ('Be always faithful to your country, Oh Magyar'). Many regular patrons had fled the Nazis, including Ferenc Molnár, one of the greatest Hungarian dramatists and novelists of the 20th century. After the fall of communism in Hungary, the city's magnificent monuments were cleansed of their Stalinist

soot, but the café's shabbiness took longer to erase because the Gerbeaud was still state owned. Now, fully restored from its tattered splendour in the 1990s, Gerbeaud is once again an elegant marble and polished brass emporium. It fills one side of a smart shopping square and spills out into the street with café tables and an ice-cream stand, one where the cones are hand-rolled. On a warm night, patrons seek out the lovely terrace situated on the quiet, tree-bedecked open square near the Danube and the Central Market.

ABOVE: Round marble tables and wicker-backed chairs have harboured clientèle of each new artistic and revolutionary movement.

OPPOSITE: The Gerbeaud, renamed the Vörösmarty under the Soviets, retains its 19th-century Art Nouveau façade.

Central Kávéház

V. KÁROLYI MIHÁLY Ú.9
BUDAPEST, HUNGARY

Central Kávéház (the Café Central), founded in 1887, closed in 1948 in the Stalinist era and reopened some 50 years later. In his 1947 autobiographical poem cycle *Grillemusik*, Lórinc Szabo pictured the café as an important workplace for the literati from the 1920s to the eve of the Second World War. Along with Kávéház New York, it became one of the most important haunts of the intelligentsia of Old Hungary. The late 19th and early 20th centuries, the twilight years of the Austro-Hungarian Empire, were its golden age.

One of the old habitués of the café remembers the Central as 'very political, smoky and loud with heated discussion'. Once when his father did not come home in time for dinner, his mother 'went looking for him at both the New York and Central cafes'.

Today the Central exudes calm splendour and a regal air. A recent visitor claimed that 'if you are there without a book, newspaper and rimmed eye glasses . . . you do feel a tad out of place'.

Among the memoirists, Zoltan Zelk has written best about the coffee-house tradition in his native city. In a sarcastic text lamenting the destruction of the coffee-house landscape during the Second World War and under Stalinist cultural policy ('the walls of bohemia have collapsed'), he sees various ghosts of the past going from the door of the Central to the revolving doors of other cafés. Among the spectres were poet Zoltan Somlyo, Ferenc Molnár and Endre Ady, as well as the editors and readers of the weekly *A Het* (The Week, 1890–1924), which was written, edited, read and debated at Café Central. Between the two world wars the café sheltered editors and collaborators of the periodical *Nyugat* (the West). Three generations of contributors wrote about Budapest's literary cafés, especially Frigyes (Friedrich) Karinthy, whose life's work was created in cafés.

Since the fall of communism, many artists who had fled have returned to Budapest. 'The birds are returning,' says native son George Lang, now an American restaurateur who, with businessman Ronald Lauder, has opened the refurbished Gundel's restaurant in Budapest. Today the Hungarian coffee-house tradition is honoured in many history books as well as in the revitalization of the old buildings.

After five decades of hibernation, the Central reawakened in the autumn of 1999 and is now beautifully refurbished. A living museum, the café easily accommodates tourists from the nearby pedestrian area of Vaci utca and locals who have visited the neighbouring market, where food vendors ply their wares in a gorgeously ornate 1897 structure.

OPPOSITE: In keeping with its name, Hungary's grand old café is centrally located and beautifully restored.

ABOVE RIGHT: Café Central was home to intellectuals and writers, including dramatist and novelist Ferenc Molnár (1878-1952).

Café Pilvax

The coffee-house tradition in Budapest, Hungary, has been closely tied to that of its Habsburg neighbour, Austria. Yet there was an anti-Austrian mood in mid-19th-century Hungary, and this was particularly manifested at Budapest's Café Pilvax (demolished in 1912), where young Hungarian intellectuals held regular round tables in the room they called the 'whispering room'. The overtly political discussions among the young revolutionaries of 1848 were led by the romantic poet Sándor Petöfi, who had set up the 'Society of Ten', a group with a thoroughly Jacobin objective. The radicals celebrated here when news arrived of the victory of the revolution in Vienna. Petöfi believed that his dream of a Hungarian republic was imminent and declared that the café was their 'Hall of Freedom'. Café Pilvax was his home until he set off from here in 1849 for the battlefield as a major in the liberation army, never to return.

Café Capsa

**CALEA VICTORIEI 36
BUCHAREST, ROMANIA**

'Capsa is the topographic and moral soul of the city,' wrote Paul Morand. The French novelist, who had visited Romania in the 1930s, devotes a chapter to 'Chez Capsa' in his *Bucarest*: 'Imagine, reunited in an apparently modest house, four old European glories: the Foyot restaurant, the Rumpelmeyer café, the Florian café in Venice and the Sacher Hotel in Vienna…

Capsa is the tympan of this great ear, that is Bucharest.'

Situated on Plata Tricolorului (Square of the Flag), the Casa Capsa opened at its present location, in the very heart of the city, in 1852. Constantin and Grigore Capsa, the Capsa brothers, bought the entire building, then called Casa Slatineanu, and opened the hotel in 1886. They gradually expanded the café and hotel to its full fame and glory.

Calea Victoriei, Bucharest's main street (roughly equivalent to the Champs-Elysées in Paris) was the first paved road in the city that became the nation's capital in the 16th century (though Vlad the Impaler mentioned its existence a century earlier). Because the Royal Library, National Theatre, Philharmonic Orchestra, and important churches and hotels were on this street, the Capsa inevitably became the central rendezvous for the leaders of society. Practically every social, political or cultural event in the country's life was to be linked in one way or another with the Casa Capsa. Most of the royal families of Europe have stayed in the hotel and visited the café, for it was this establishment that organized imperial, royal and princely dinners, weddings and balls, and introduced French cuisine to the country.

Parliamentary and constitutional debates and negotiations were conducted at Capsa; here politicians made peace after endless conflicts. It became the privileged meeting place of all the writers, poets, actors and musicians who counted in the country, including foreign artists who performed in Romania,

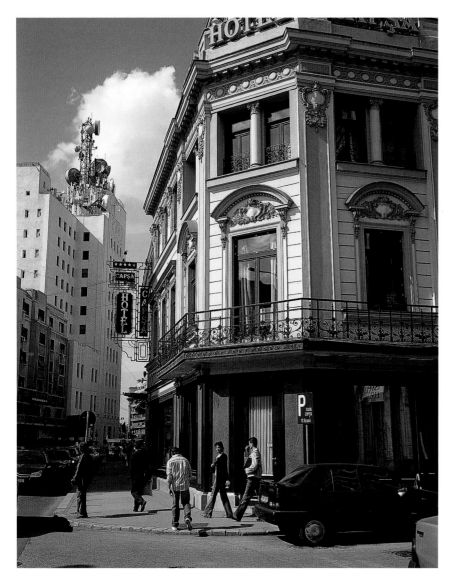

LEFT & OPPOSITE: This elegant aristocratic hotel, café, and neoclassical restaurant is celebrated in many novels as the meeting place for foreign dignitaries, such as Sarah Bernhardt, and native writers, such as Mihai Eminescu.

such as Sarah Bernhardt, Eugène Ysaÿe, and Réjane.

The heyday of the café lasted from the Belle Époque until the years after the First World War. It received prominent mention in the works of Ion Luca Caragiale, author and director of the National Theatre until 1912, and from Cezar Petrescu, a prolific novelist whose *Calea Victoriei* (1929) depicts the tumultuous, stressful life of the city. The latter was also the founder of *The Thinker*, an expression of the traditionalist movement that flourished in the 1930s. In her Balkan trilogy (1960–66), English novelist Olivia Manning described the Café Capsa as it was during the Second World War.

Among frequent visitors to Café Capsa were the poets Mihai Eminescu (1850–89), considered Europe's last Romantic poet, and Tudor Arghezi, and world-renowned composer George Enescu. The painters Amman, Nicolae Grigorescu and Ion Tuculescu, and important literary critics Titu Maiorescu and George Calinescu were regular patrons. To be or not to be part of the cultural debates at Capsa meant to be or not to be recognized as belonging to the country's intelligentsia.

After many years of decay during the communist regime, Capsa's glamour was finally restored, along with the hotel's 61 elegant rooms, and the café reopened in 2003. These days, Café Capsa remains an ornate and expensive coffee-house, occasionally empty of people, but always richly filled with the cultural and literary history of Bucharest. Today, in the words of a local resident, 'the tympan of Bucharest has moved north a few blocks to the Athene Palace Hotel, simply referred to as 'The Hilton'. However, another resident insists the Capsa remains 'cosy' and 'chic.'

Central House of Writers

BOLSHAYA NIKITSKAYA UL. 53
MOSCOW, RUSSIA

The coffee trade to Russia from the Middle East began as early as the 17th century, but the coffee-house tradition itself came later, lasting from 1835 until the Bolshevik Revolution, when it was compromised by communist rule. Before the Soviet era, the Central House of Writers stood proudly. It was described by Tolstoy in his epic novel, *War and Peace* (1865–69). The most important Russian writer usually associated with Moscow (rather than St Petersburg), he was a frequent visitor.

During the revolutionary days of October 1917, in dozens of small coffee parlours in Moscow and St Petersburg, men wearing red armbands and carrying rifles warmed themselves over their coffee. In the

BELOW: The neoclassical architecture of this grand street of official buildings includes the House of Writers, where visiting world writers are entertained.

Soviet government institution, the Central House of Writers inevitably betrayed the tradition of the coffee-houses as a refuge of free thought. Today, reborn, it pays homage to the cafés of earlier years by echoing, in one of its small café rooms, an older tradition of café walls being painted by artists – a tradition embodied in the Café Pittoresque (1918), no longer extant. A dozen artists had participated in the design of this earlier café, for their goal was to have a site that reflected all the arts: literature, theatre, painting and architecture. Their efforts were overtaken by political events, as shown in the changing name of the café, which had been the Red Cockerel in 1917, and then changed again under the Bolsheviks to Café of the Revolutionary City.

Before the Soviet era, artists' cafés still proliferated in the city. Futurists from Western Europe came here to various centres of the avant-garde, including the Poets' Café, Café Domino and Café Pegasus Stall (as well as to St Petersburg's Stray Dog Café, described below). It was at the Poets' Café that Vladimir Mayakovsky (*The Bedbug*, 1928) gathered the Futurists around him 'like Robin Hood and his band of robbers'. Ulla Heise describes these Russian 'cafés', where little coffee (or any food, for that matter) was available: often a simple room with chairs and tables, the bare necessities. Ilya Ehrenburg (*The Thaw*, 1954), who later

ABOVE: Moscow's House of Writers often entertains small delegations and, in its larger dining rooms, both official and private parties.

grander cafés, where there were gambling rooms, they placed and took bets – as did revolutionaries in the cafés of Berlin and Vienna – on how long the new government would retain power.

The Soviet regime turned this grand café into an official meeting place for the nation's politically acceptable writers. In becoming an official moved to Paris, describes the walls of the Poets' Café as 'embellished with grotesque paintings and no less grotesque inscriptions'.

In stark contrast to the poorest of these early 20th-century artists' cafés, the Central House of Writers is in the grand tradition. Located in a 19th-century mansion, it is the most elegant of the houses for Russian writers. Its grand interior, with chandeliers, oriental carpets, and large meeting and dining areas, offered an impressive welcome to foreign artists and state visitors. A club for the Soviet Writers' Union, exclusive to the politically acceptable during Soviet rule, it served as a location for writers' receptions, poetry readings and film showings. In the ground-floor rooms, the ceilings are beamed with wood.

With the end of the Soviet Union, the Central House of Writers was opened to all (all, that is, who could afford it) and continued to welcome foreign writers and official events. Legend has it that this palatial building was the model for 'Griboyedov House', described in great detail in Mikhail Bulgakov's *The Master and Margarita* (1967). The villa still has magnificent chandeliers in the entrance hall, as well as some of the most beautiful dining rooms in Moscow, a portrait gallery, a restaurant and cafés. These days the Central House stages events that often attract huge celebrity audiences. The private rooms host literary soirées, and the dining rooms are rented out to groups of foreign travellers. Earlier, France's André Gide and other members of the leading world authors' organization, PEN, gathered here.

Russia's own Yevgeny Yevtushenko and Andrei Voznesensky have read here along with visiting fellow poets from western Europe. Yevtushenko's semi-autobiographical, post-Soviet work *Don't Die Before You're Dead* is an account of the 1991 triumph of Boris Yeltsin (Yevtushenko served in the Soviet parliament from 1988 to 1991).

LEFT: Vladimir Mayakowsky (1893–1930) began writing poetry before he was arrested and jailed in 1909. When released in 1912, he moved to St. Petersburg and, with his circle, founded Russian Futurism, read poetry in the streets and attacked the bourgeois art establishment. For a time Mayakowsky was the leading poet of the Bolshevik Revolution of 1917 and of the early Soviet period. There is now a V. V. Mayakowsky Museum in Moscow.

LEFT: Drawings on the wall of the café on the lower floor, echo the now-defunct Poets' Café in which Futurist artists filled each wall with their drawings and poems.

St Petersburg (called Leningrad in the Soviet era) has been immortalized in the fiction of Pushkin, Gogol, Dostoevsky, Turgenev and Biely. Built at the behest of Tsar Peter the Great in 1703, this grand city rapidly became both the political and administrative capital of Russia and the country's cultural and intellectual centre, until Moscow usurped both these functions.

A strong Italian and French influence can be seen in St

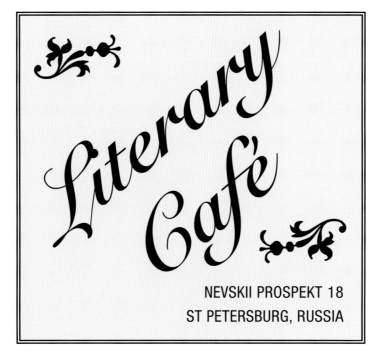

Literary Café

**NEVSKII PROSPEKT 18
ST PETERSBURG, RUSSIA**

Petersburg's architecture, including this café, which was founded in 1835 as the confectionery Wolff et Berange. The Literaturnoe Kafe, as it subsequently became, has presided over literary events on Nevskii Prospekt in St Petersburg for some 150 years.

The three-mile long central avenue was praised by Gogol, in his famous story 'Nevsky Prospect', as 'gay' and 'brilliant' – but, he wrote, 'I always wrap myself up more closely in my cloak when I walk along it.' Andrey Bely (*Petersburg*, 1916) adds: 'A Petersburg street in autumn is piercing; it both chills you to the marrow and tickles.' Dostoevsky's narrator in *Notes from the Underground* strolls the street with 'countless torments, disparagements, and outbursts of spleen', dodging 'horse guards officers or hussars, or fine ladies'. By contrast, the French writer Alexandre Dumas (*Travels across Russia*) called it 'the street of religious tolerance' because there were so many churches of differing religions.

The Literary Café was a favourite haunt of Alexander Pushkin, Russia's first national poet, best known probably for the novel-in-verse *Eugene Onegin* (1825–31). It was here in the early days of 1837 that he spent his last hour with his second before departing for his fatal duel with d'Anthes, the French nobleman whom he had accused of being the lover of his young and flirtatious wife. In that extravagantly romantic gesture of a

LEFT: The entrance plaque honours more than a century of Russian writers, beginning with Pushkin, who have walked through the Literary Café's door. Pushkin spent his last hour here (when it was called Wolff et Berange) before his fatal duel.

OPPOSITE: The Literary Café is situated near the canal, which freezes over in the winter months, and centrally located on Nevskii Prospekt, St Petersburg's grand avenue.

OPPOSITE: The Literary Café's newly renovated dining area, with wallpaper that looks like a library of Russian volumes honoring Dostoevsky and the other writers who haunted this café.

challenge to a duel, the poet who had established Russia's modern literary language brought about his own end.

Another café patron was the writer and critic Belinsky (an early champion both of Dostoevsky and of the realist Gogol), who died in stark poverty in 1848 at the age of 37. Fyodor Dostoevsky himself, who would become a towering figure in world literature, first came to St Petersburg to study military engineering, which he soon abandoned for literature. His first work was published in 1846. After an agonizing period of exile in Siberia, to which he was sentenced for revolutionary activity, Dostoevsky returned to St Petersburg (and the Literaturnoe Kafe) a changed man, to write, among

other works, *Notes from the Underground*, *Crime and Punishment* (set in St Petersburg), and *The Brothers Karamazov*. He died and was buried in the city in 1881. Today there is a dark little underground café or bar called 'The Idiot' in his honour, where they claim to have his typewriter.

History books and mid-19th-century guidebooks list the Literaturnoe Kafe (Literary Café), or a room in the café, as the 'Wolff et Berange' and the 'Café Chinois'. Late in the 19th century, the second-floor salon hosted literary evenings, and sketches of famous writers still decorate the wall. A café by day, the Literaturnoe becomes more of a restaurant at night, and recent renovations have lamentably obliterated much of its threadbare old-world charm.

The Stray
Dog

ISSKUSTV SQUARE 5
ST PETERSBURG, RUSSIA

Brodiachaia Sobaka (The Stray Dog), its name suggesting camaraderie in exile, was legendary as home to St Petersburg's avant-garde intelligentsia in the Silver Age (the Golden Age being that of Pushkin). They met for five brief but intense years from 1911 to 1915 in what was then a semi-private club or art cabaret, probably the vaulted wine cellar of a progressive aristocrat named Boris Pronin, who was part of the shimmering era's creative and intellectual life. Pre-revolutionary artists and writers in attendance included poet and dramatist Vladimir Mayakovsky (*The Bedbug*), Symbolist poet Alexander Blok, and Sergey Esenin, author of 'Moscow of the Taverns' (1924). Composers such as Arthur Lourie

BELOW: The Stray Dog is 'underground', where subversive artistic and political thought brewed in the early 20th century.

ABOVE: Two scenes of the present Stray Dog café and cabaret where today's actors and artists honour the earlier Russian artists, particularly Vladimir Mayakowsky, poet Alexander Blok, and the Acmeist poets.

performed their latest avant-garde works here.

The Acmeist poets, including Nikolai Gumilev and Osip Mandelstam, were the dominant members of the Brodiachaia Sobaka circle. Acmeists wrote lucid, carefully crafted verse, reacting against murky *fin de siècle* Symbolism. Their *grande dame*, the most famous patron of the café, was Anna Akhmatova (1889–1966) – 'We are all sinners here.' Her second book of poetry (*The Rosary*, 1914) brought her fame and eventually cult figure status. She had an affair with the composer Lourie, who set her poetry to music (he eventually fled to Berlin, then Paris). A later love affair with the composer Shostakovich also inspired mutual artistic tributes. Her purported fling with the then 35-year-old British philosopher and diplomat Isaiah Berlin (Akhmatova was 55 at the time), as well as her reactionary Acmeist poetry, led to her denunciation by Stalin ('Russia… Under the wheels of Black Marias,' she wrote). For generations

afterwards she influenced young poets, most recently Joseph Brodsky, who won a Nobel Prize for Literature in 1987.

The Brodiachaia Sobaka was closed by the authorities in 1915 but has now reopened. In its large back room one can find actors fervently arguing or rehearsing for theatrical performances, among them Sergei Kolesnikov, who is also a passionate historian of the café. Old photos of early 20th-century literary and theatrical legends hang on the brick walls. A recent book authored by Sergei Shults called *The Stray Dog* (2003) narrates in detail the saga of the café.

In spirit and décor, the Brodiachaia Sobaka remains today an unadorned and plain gathering place for those dedicated to art, literature and the underground spirit. Taking advantage of the new freedoms now available in Russia, the artists here have renewed the flame first kindled almost 100 years ago.

RIGHT: The back room of the Stray Dog is where poets read and theatre is performed. The furniture is functional, the ceilings low, but the aspirations of the artistic clientèle are high.

**HOTEL GRAND
KARL JOHANS GATE 31
OSLO, NORWAY**

With the opening of the Grand Hotel in 1874 the Grand Café became Oslo's main restaurant, a status it retained for many years. Refurbished and expanded in the 1890s, it was a favourite haunt of artists and intellectuals. The great playwright Henrik Ibsen sat at his regular table here every day. (In his time it was called the Kristiana: Oslo changed its own name to Christiana, then Kristiana, and back to Oslo in 1925.) The hotel, and its café, occupy a key location on Oslo's main street, Karl Johans Gate.

Ibsen (1828–1916) had returned to Norway in 1891 after 27 years of exile in Italy and Germany. He quickly came into conflict with the intellectual establishment, though the arguments did not take place in the Grand Café. (Knut Hamsun, the county's great prose writer, had attacked him at a public lecture, at which Ibsen was present.) But Ibsen remained a respected regular guest at the Grand; his wife noted that he continued 'the custom he had adopted in southern Europe – a daily visit to his favourite café. In Rome, it had been the Café Tritone, in Munich the Café Maximilian,

and in Kristiana it was the Grand Café.' He visited every day at 2pm, so punctually that people said they could set their clocks by his arrival. It is reported that American, English, German and French tourists often came to catch a glimpse of the famous playwright, and there are countless stories and anecdotes about Ibsen at the café. The author of *A Doll's House* (1879), *The Wild Duck* (1884), *Hedda Gabler* (1890) and *The Master Builder* (1892) became perhaps the most influential playwright of the 20th century.

Edvard Munch was just one of many painters who made the Grand Café their gathering place. His painting of the café is called *Henrik Ibsen at the Grand Café, 1898*. Munch (1863–1944) is Norway's one giant of the visual arts. Early in the century he led Europe into the new world of German Expressionism, and upon his return to his native land from Germany in 1909, he found a temporary escape from his anxious world at the café. In his best-known canvas, *The Scream*, the artist distorts reality to create an intensely personal vision of anguish and fear. The Munch Museum is at Toyengata 53.

Other frequent café guests among the artists and intellectuals included writer Hans Jæger, sculptor Gustav Vigeland, and artists Oda and

ABOVE: This dining area set for evening fare displays the elegant furnishings that aptly illustrate the name of this Norwegian café, founded in 1874.

RIGHT: Norway's most famous painter, Edvard Munch; with the exception of Ibsen, he was the most renowned patron of the Grand Café.

OPPOSITE: Its location on Oslo's main street leading from the castle helps to ensure the continuity of the venerable Grand Café.

Christian Krohg. The large mural at one end of the café, painted by their son Per Krohg in 1928 and installed in 1932, portrays the café and its guests, including Ibsen and Munch, as though in the 1890s. Though Ibsen's table and chair were removed long ago to a museum, there is a plaque in the corner where he presided for so many years.

As artists returned to Norway from the big cities on the continent to the south, the café became a hub of cultural exchange of fresh new ideas and bohemian lifestyles. Free and open, worldly wise, active and full of energy, the returnees sought to revolutionize Norwegian artistic life. They wanted to depict Norwegian nature and Norwegian society in a way that would make people open their eyes.

Once the social centre for Oslo's artistic elite, today the Grand has gone back to the bourgeoisie, and newer pavement cafés have sprung up along the tree-lined thoroughfare of Karl Johans Gate.

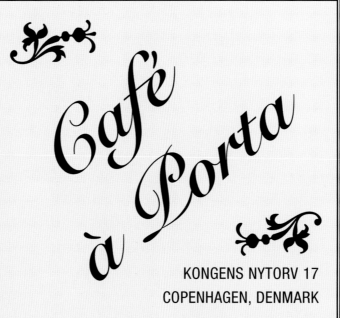

**KONGENS NYTORV 17
COPENHAGEN, DENMARK**

Founded by the Swiss immigrant Stephan à Porta in 1857, Café à Porta is still here and remains well known for its elegant interior. A Porta had taken over an old café and bakery dating from 1788, demolished the building and built the five-storey house as we see it today, designed by the architect of the Tivoli, H. C. Stilling. There is a restaurant one flight up. Because the café faces the Royal Theatre on what was once the central square of Copenhagen, it has long been a meeting place of dramatists and actors, including Olaf Poulsen, who ate there daily.

Copenhagen, with a thousand years of history, is the largest city in Scandinavia. A Porta's most famous patron was the storyteller Hans Christian Andersen (1805–75), beloved author of such stories as 'The Little Mermaid', 'The Emperor's New Clothes' and 'The Ugly Duckling'. From 1866 to 1869 Andersen lived two floors above the café and had his own seat in the third salon.

In the 1880s and 1890s, when Copenhagen cafés reached their zenith as meeting places for writers and leading citizens, all sorts of writers, critics, journalists, actors, artists and curious onlookers frequented the café. Writer and critic Georg Brandes was a patron after 1870, when not travelling the continent. Karen Blixen ('Isak Dinesen', 1885–1962), author of 'Babette's Feast' and the autobiographical *Out of Africa*, was a regular here as well as at Café Bernina (now gone).

Between-the-war regulars included three dramatists: Kaj Munk, a parson living in western Jutland whose moralizing plays revived Danish drama in the 1930s; the notable anti-fascist Kjeld Abell; and the

LEFT: The modest entrance to this multi-storied café and restaurant, a favourite with the great fairy tale writer Hans Christian Anderson, belies its elegant interior.

OPPOSITE: The restaurant is located on the first floor and looks down on Denmark's Royal Theatre, attracting after-theatre diners and actors.

Café Bernina

Copenhagen's Café Bernina was founded in 1881 and survived until around 1928. Its heyday lasted from the 1880s to the 1910s. Bohemian in character, it was a meeting place for writers from Norway and Sweden who were drawn to Copenhagen during the Modern Breakthrough Movement (1870–1900) – among them the Swedish-born writer Hjalmar Söderberg (*Doktor Glas*, 1905), who settled in Copenhagen – and for the left-wing students and academics who met in the nearby Students' Association. The latter gathered around the Danish liberal critic Georg Brandes, considered to be the greatest European critic since Taine and a major influence on realism in Scandinavian literature and on James Joyce's Shakespeare theories. Among Brandes' many works is the six-volume *Main Currents of Nineteenth-Century Literature* (1872–91).

Among other devotees of Café Bernina were the 1890s group of Symbolist writers, centred on the Catholic poet Johannes Jorgensen, and one of Denmark's first feminist novelists, Agnes Henningsen. Her son, Denmark's liberal critic and poet Poul Henningsen, became famous for his hanging lamp which took the first prize at the Paris World Exhibition 1925. Karen Blixen, who wrote under the pseudonym Isak Dinesen, was a regular, as were the first generation of Danish film-makers grouped around the silent movie entrepreneur Ole Olsen during the First World War. In his memoirs, *The Legend of My Life*, Jorgensen describes drinking here with Norwegian author Knut Hamsun, who was on one of his 'Bacchic tours' followed by 'a crowd of fauns and satyrs and young nymphs'.

ABOVE: The ground floor of Café à Porta looks out at all the bicycles parked in a square that was once the heart of the city. Its central location draws students and tourists, as well as dramatists, actors, and writers.

early Existentialist dramatist Carl Erik Soya. In 1936 James Joyce came to Café à Porta with Denmark's then celebrity writer Tom Kristensen.

During the German occupation in the 1940s, the café remained open despite dwindling supplies of coffee and tea. After a brief period as an Italian restaurant, it was renovated in 1961 and restored under the supervision of a conservationist, who added carpet and panelling.

Wintergarten Café

LITERATURHAUS
FASANENSTRASSE 23
BERLIN, GERMANY

Once a centre of the coffee-house tradition, by the early 20th century Berlin had lost most of its great old cafés, such as the Romanisches Café and Café Stehely. Remaining today is the Wintergarten Café im Literaturhaus for artists, sponsored by the city council, which is in a 19th-century villa located near the famous Kurfürstendamm and beside the Kollwitz Museum. Within this building there are a restaurant, a library, a conservatory (with an iron and glass ceiling) and, in the basement, a very good literary bookshop. The café, with its long bar, ochre walls, and high gilt stucco ceilings, has a garden which is open in warm weather.

Germany's *Literaturhäuser* ('houses of literature') are linked in a network

BELOW: One enters the café up a flight of stairs and through a garden, where today's writers enjoy coffee and read the paper on Sunday mornings.

Berlin's Other Cafés

Another Berlin café worthy of mention is the old Café Einstein Stammhaus at Kurfürstenstrasse 58, where the writers of the 1920s gathered. Opened in an 1898 villa as a Viennese-style coffee-house with music (one of its owners was from Vienna), the Einstein today features Italian coffee served in an elegant room. After the fall of the Berlin Wall, the owners opened another Café Einstein on Unter den Linden in the former East Berlin.

Today's writers, artists and politicians use the Paris Bar (Kantstrasse 152) as their watering hole. Actors fill the chairs during the Berlin Film Festival. While there are no free newspapers, Paris Bar can boast an array of modern art on the walls. Illustrator Michel Würthle draws here as an habitué. He studied painting in Vienna and is a world traveller and bohemian who took over the journal *Exiles*. The bar was apparently founded by a soldier, who wanted to create a miniature of Paris's La Coupole with a corner café.

Romanisches Café, Berlin

The greatest literary café in Berlin among those that have closed and disappeared into history is the Romanisches Café.

In this barn-like structure, which could accommodate nearly a thousand patrons, Expressionist artist George Grosz would appear dressed as an American cowboy in boots and spurs; the great world chess champion Emmanuel Lasker played at a row of tables in the balcony. Its heyday was the golden age of the German 1920s. Bertolt Brecht had moved back to Berlin from Munich and Thomas Mann was writing; illustrious immigrants included Franz Kafka, Stephan Zweig and British poet Christopher Isherwood. When Polish poet A. N. Stencl discovered all his friends at the Romanisches, he was 'simply drunk with joy'. He had coffee and a soft-boiled egg in a glass, the usual Romanisches fare. 'Berlin gobbled up talents and human energies with unexampled appetite,' wrote playwright Carl Zuckmayer. 'Out of the Romanische came many a novel that is now considered classic; many a play that is still performed; movie scripts that still move us; [and] a surfeit of articles in Berlin's magazines, noted chroniclers of the period Von Eckardt and Gilman.

Almost every prominent writer in the Western world came to Berlin at one time or another during the 1920s. Among the transients were writers in Yiddish and literati displaced from Odessa, Kiev, Warsaw and Vilna by pogroms and wars.

(www.literaturhaus.net) and are located in Basel, Berlin, Cologne, Frankfurt, Hamburg, Munich, Salzburg and Stuttgart (in order of founding). These establishments award literary prizes, offer readings by authors, house small bookshops, and host poetry jams and lectures.

In the years after the Second World War the 'Gruppe 47' (see sidebar page 102) met in the Wintergarten several times to read and discuss their work in progress. Though membership of the group varied, as did its place of meeting in Germany, among the authors were the novelists Günter Grass, Martin Walser and Heinrich Böll, the left-wing poet Hans Magnus Enzensberger and the dramatist Peter Handke. Gruppe 47 disbanded in the late 1960s.

Young writers today frequently have breakfast at the Wintergarten Café, where they can read a variety of newspapers.

ABOVE: The coffee bar, which is less conducive to reading, is favoured by Berlin's youth. The fixtures may be modern, but the traditional glass display case and coffee machine have a lengthy tradition.

OPPOSITE: The Wintergarten's large café one floor up is comfortable and often quiet enough for reading. The Literaturhaus schedule is a full programme of recitals and readings.

Kaffeebaum

KLEINE FLEISCHERGASSE 4
LEIPZIG, GERMANY

'The Arab Coffee Tree' ('Zum Arabischen Coffebaum' is carved above the door) was probably the first coffee-house to open in Leipzig, the home base of Johann Sebastian Bach, Felix Mendelssohn and, more recently, the conductor Kurt Masur. Leipzig, one of the bastions of the German Enlightenment, has always been the centre of the German book trade. Thus it is to be expected that this city would be fertile ground for the coffee-house culture, and that German writers and publishers would have long come to the Kaffeebaum.

The house is characterized by a 1719 Baroque frieze above the centre door of a Turk sitting under a coffee tree, handing a bowl of coffee to a cherub. As the door was probably built about 1500, some proclaim the establishment the oldest

coffee-house in the world, or at least the oldest coffee-house outside of the Arab world and the oldest still existing. One source says there was a coffee bar here in 1695, before it was christened 'The Arab Coffee Tree'. All agree that by 1700 Leipzig had become a centre for coffee-milling and the production of packaging.

Among the illustrious patrons who walked through the coffee-tree door were professor and literary critic Johann Christoph Gottsched, one of the powerful influences on 18th-century German literature, and poet and moralist Christian Gellert (who taught Lessing and Goethe here). Patrons included Lessing and Goethe themselves, and also Napoleon Bonaparte. Goethe lived in Leipzig from 1765 to 1768 and set a key scene in his *Faust* in 'Auerbach's Cellar', which made the Kaffeebaum's cellar famous. Gottsched, editor and author of *Der Biedermann* (the oppositional publication of the early Leipzig Enlightenment), signed his first article on 1 March 1728 with the coffee-house address (referring to it as Lehmannische Coffee-house, after the owner).

The first club of German journalists met between 1745 and 1748 and published the journal *Bremer Beiträge*. Ten members of this group (which was of a literary more than a patriotic bent), including the Schlegel brothers, founders of the journal *Athenaeum* and the initiators and theorists of German Romanticism, gathered at a café regularly. Though there is no written record of precisely which café they met in, historians believe it was the Kaffeebaum. Among numerous other great patrons of the café were the poet

ABOVE: On the ground floor is a large café room with round tables for conversation and regular meetings.

OPPOSITE, LEFT: Under the door's Baroque frieze have walked Lessing, Goethe, Liszt, and Wagner. The outdoor seating is a recent convenience for summer days.

OPPOSITE, RIGHT: In the upstairs museum, wall paintings and mannequins underline the central position of music in the café's history.

ABOVE: One of several coffee rooms in the Kaffeebaum, home for Leipzig's pioneers in music, literature, and journalism since the 18th century.

them in the Kaffeebaum in 1833. He wrote a series of piano pieces in 1837 named 'Davidsbündlertänze'. The group established and published the *Neue Zeitschrift für Musik*, laying the foundations for music criticism in Germany.

The importance of the coffee-house tradition in Germany was celebrated in 1901 in the *Leipziger Tageblatt*: 'Germania's sons sit drinking their coffee [where] literature has found its salvation in the coffee-house and with it its exponents. There the army of collaborators and review writers ogle each other and the journalists.'

Appropriately, the Kaffeebaum has established a museum, probably the only dedicated coffee museum in Germany. The curator, Hannelore Stingl, in 2003 published an illustrated history of the café. At one time the café also had billiard rooms, for during the 18th century every coffee-house proprietor in Leipzig took out a permit for billiards. On the upper floor are cafés in three different styles: French, Arabic and Viennese.

In another room, called the Leipziger Künstlercafé, the city's publishers meet regularly in closed session; here too launch parties for new books are held (microphones are provided). This linking of the café with a city's bookselling trade is an even stronger and more organized association than one finds in Paris's Brasserie Lipp.

The café underwent a major renovation in the late 1990s and now the coffee tree flowers once more. This legendary café with its Baroque over-the-door frieze preserves its history while serving the new, post-Cold War Germany.

Friedrich Klopstock (who influenced Goethe), the pianist and teacher Johann Cramer, the socialist August Bebel (a founder of the Social Democratic Party), and the communist Karl Liebknecht.

This café also played a significant role in music history, for here one might have met the composers Franz Liszt, Robert Schumann and Richard Wagner. The so-called 'Davidsbündler' group gathered here around Schumann, who convened

Café Luitpold

BRIENNERSTRASSE 11
MUNICH, GERMANY

Opened in 1888, and named in his honour with the 'most gracious permission' of the sovereign Prince Regent of Bavaria, Café Luitpold was built in the palatial Wittelsbach style. Many proclaimed this the finest café in Germany, of equal merit to Paris's Café de la Paix. The Palm Court's (Palmengarten's) glass-domed ceiling and hanging plants and palms attracted Henrik Ibsen, Johann Strauss Junior and members of the royal court of Bavaria. Today, standing amid a shopping complex, it attracts well-dressed Munich citizens and tourists.

Like the Café Central in Vienna, the Luitpold attracted both young aristocrats and members of the art world. In 1911 art history was made in this café with the genesis there of the Blaue Reiter ('Blue Rider') school of artists.

BELOW: The Luitpold, which opened in 1888, was Munich's attempt to match the cafés of Paris and Vienna. Spacious with a patisserie in the centre and tables extending into an inner courtyard, its patrons have included Arnold Schoenberg, Paul Klee, and Wassily Kandinsky.

Among its founders were Wassily Kandinsky (whose painting *Le cavalier bleu* gave the group its name), Franz Marc and the art dealer Hans Goltz. Other members included Alfred Kubin, August Macke, Paul Klee and Arnold Schoenberg – the last of whom, of course, would achieve fame chiefly as a composer. The Expressionist movement, which this group set in motion, became dominant in the European art world before the First World War; but the Blaue Reiter group disbanded in 1914, and Marc and Macke were killed in the conflict.

The now renowned Austrian Expressionist painter and draftsman Egon Schiele, who died in 1918 at just 28 years of age, had his first German exhibition here. The Luitpold is also where the founders of the satiric magazine *Simplicissimus* (1896–1944) gathered, though some maintain that they may at times have preferred the modest Alter Simpl in Türkenstrasse. Albert Langen was the first editor.

The Luitpold faced its greatest challenge during the devastating bombings of the Second World War, but in the decades since it has been revived, reopening in 2003 with new décor. A fancier café now, it features an adjoining gallery – a room inaugurated by an exhibition devoted to the original café.

ABOVE: One of the founders of the Blue Rider group of painters in Café Luitpold was Russian-born Wassily Kandinsky (1866-1944), an abstract painter and theorist who espoused vibrant colour. He moved to Munich when he was 30 years of age.

A Postwar Call for Renewal of German Literature

Like Spain's 'Generation of '98' after their country's humiliation in the Spanish–American War of 1898, in 1947 German poets called for a renewal of literature and society in the wake of the Second World War. It was from Munich that Hans Magnus Enzensberger and Alfred Andersch issued their invitation to the first meeting of what was to become 'Gruppe 47' in their journal *Der Ruf* (The Call): 'We are a "Café Central" of a literature that has no capital city,' said Enzensberger. Gruppe 47 met occasionally at Munich's Literaturhaus, as well as in other major cities. Today the Literaturhaus (Salvatorplatz 1) houses the Café Dukatz, a primary venue for the city's literary readings, events and exhibitions. Gruppe 47's most vital years were between 1958 and 1963. Thereafter the group splintered into small numbers prior to its demise in 1967.

Munich's Other Cafés

Munich has a rich literary past. The Crocodile Society was a literary association begun in 1856 at the initiation of the Bavarian king, Maximilian II, who summoned chosen writers to Munich and paid their keep. They met consecutively in three cafés: first the Café Stadt München (1856–57), then the Café Daburger, and from 1883 the Café Dall'Armi. This circle included Emanuel Geibel, Professor of Literature and Lecturer Royal; Professor of Legal History Felix Dahn (who had been a member of the 'Tunnel' group in Leipzig); Adolf F. von Schack, writer, translator and diplomat; and Paul Heyse, 1910 Nobel Laureate in Literature and master of the short story.

In the years before the First World War, younger artists and left-wing bohemians met in the Café Stefanie, challenging the Expressionist establishment that reigned in Café Luitpold. Stefan George, Frank Wedekind and Erich Muehsam met at the Stefanie, which gained the nickname of Café Groessenwahn ('Megalomania'). In the Café Extrablatt, which closed in 1997, novelist Patrick Suskind (*Das Parfüm*) was a regular customer, as was poet Wolf Wondratschef. Today media people and writers meet at Schumanns Bar (almost as famous as Berlin's Paris Bar).

ABOVE: Because of the important role of art in the history of the Luitpold, its gallery features art exhibitions and photographs of the historical building before the World War II bombing.

Café Américain

**HOTEL AMERICAN
LEIDSEKADE 97
AMSTERDAM, THE NETHERLANDS**

The world-famous Hotel American – the façade in a Dutch version of Art Nouveau created in 1882 – was designed by Willem Kromhout. The café has long been a gathering place for exiles and a haunt of artists. Its Art Deco interior has been preserved right down to the vaulted ceilings, leaded stained-glass windows and lighting. The murals, already more than 80 years old, depict scenes from Shakespeare's *A Midsummer Night's Dream*. The Hotel American is located on a canal in the city centre, adjacent to the Stadsschouwburg Theatre and so convenient for opera and ballet.

Klaus Mann, son of the Nobel Prize-winning novelist Thomas Mann, left Germany in 1933 to live in Amsterdam, where he edited the anti-Nazi journal *Sammlung*. At the café here Mann met Menno

OPPOSITE: Both the café and hotel were rebuilt at the turn of the 19th century by architect W. Kromhout in Art Nouveau style, with leaded windows, sculptures, and decorative arched ceilings and furnishings.

RIGHT: The lamps and murals date from the Art Deco 1920s and the centre island for coffee machine, flowers, and pastry give the large coffee establishment a sense of intimacy. The hotel and café have recently been restored.

Amsterdam's Other Cafés

Café de Zwart, two doors up from the old Café Luxembourg, on a square featuring the famous Athenaeum bookstore and news centre, has usurped the role once played by the Américain and is now known as 'the writers' café'.

One of the new waterfront cafés is the VOC, an acronym for the name in Dutch of the coffee-importing Dutch East India Company – the Dutch having been the first in Europe (after the Portuguese and Spanish) to look beyond their borders to conquer as well as expand trade by founding major coffee companies. The café is also popular with North Americans because Henrik Hudson launched his epic voyage near here.

Café Hoppe, one of the oldest coffee-houses in the Netherlands (founded 1670), has remained a gathering place for a variety of artists, as are also Café Welling, Café-Restaurant Dantzig (popular during the Second World War and 50 metres from the opera house), J. W. Brouwersstraat (near the Concertgebouw), and two trendy cafés called De Jaren and the De Engelbewaarder Literary Café.

The coffee-house tradition has undergone one particular change in swinging Amsterdam, where cannabis 'coffee shops' are now tolerated. Some tourists may be surprised to find on 'coffee shop' menus a variety of weed listed alongside the selection of coffees (if, indeed, coffee is served at all). The innovation makes for a strange contrast between the elegance of the older coffee-houses and today's casually dressed, pot-smoking patrons.

ABOVE: The decorated tile floor matches the arched ceilings. The palm trees and indirect lighting warm the angles of the tables and paintings.

ter Braak (1902–40), who played an important role in the debate around émigré literature and fought all forms of fascism and national socialism. As a leading Dutch social philosopher, he had founded the literary monthly *Forum* and would later found the Comite van Waakzaamheid (Committee of Watchfulness). He became known as 'the conscience of Dutch literature'. When Germany invaded The Netherlands in 1940, he committed suicide. He was just 38 years old.

The Café Américain, the most prestigious in Amsterdam, has been restored, though since about 1980 it has ceased to be a haunt for the literati.

Café Royal

**68 REGENT STREET
LONDON, ENGLAND**

'There is no instinct in the Englishman to be companionable in public,' declared English Symbolist poet Arthur Symons, who did more than any other figure of the *fin de siècle* to interpret French culture and literature for his countrymen. His friend and fellow poet Ernest Dowson added: 'In London we cannot read our poems to one another, as they do in Paris.' The place that above all helped to overcome this perceived English reticence was the Café Royal. 'If you want to see English people at their most English,' said actor-manager Sir Herbert Beerbohm Tree, 'go to the Café Royal where they are trying their hardest to be French.' More avant-garde than academic, the Café Royal attracted a clientèle of princes and peers as well as of the leading lights of literature. Its heyday was between the 1880s and the beginning of the Second World War in 1939.

The Café Royal began in 1863 as a tiny eating-house in Glasshouse Street (Café Restaurant Nicols), moving to its present glamorous site two years later. When Regent Street was rebuilt, so was the building now housing the Café Royal, which grew into a multi-storey institution with a Grill Room known for its French cuisine, a billiard room, and grand banqueting rooms (among the extravagant events hosted here was one expensive banquet held in honour of the sculptor Auguste Rodin). The National Sporting Club still meets here, as

RIGHT: The greatest writers of the second half of the 19th century passed through the Café Royal's Regent Street entrance lobby.

ABOVE: One of the many upstairs private dining rooms of England's most venerable literary establishment, Café Royal.

LEFT: Oscar Wilde (1854–1900) and Lord Alfred ('Bosie') Douglas (1870–1945), his lover. They caused a scandal after a lawsuit Wilde brought against Douglas's father, the Marquess of Queensbury, who had accused Wilde of sodomy.

do a Masonic Lodge and the numerous other groups renting the banquet rooms.

The 'N' on the entrance floor with the crown insignia refers not to Napoleon but to 'Nicols' – the original owner, Daniel Nicols Thevenon. Beyond the elegant door one enters a veritable palace of etched glass, bevelled mirrors and carved wood. The dining room has been described as a jewel of Edwardian decadence, with hand-painted ceilings depicting mythological scenes.

The list of habitués of the Royal reads like a pantheon of European literature, including notably the aesthetes and poets of the 1890s: French poets Verlaine and Rimbaud quarrelled here; Arthur Symons recalled 'the hot nights and the heated noons' of the domino room; Frank Harris, George Moore, and Aubrey Beardsley (who played the house piano) brought their *risqué* reputations here. Other celebrity patrons included Arnold Bennett, Arthur Conan Doyle, G. K. Chesterton, Augustus John, Shaw, Whistler, and W.B. Yeats. Indeed, according to Virginia Nicholson, 'If August John was there (and he usually was) he could be relied upon to foot the bill.' The Café Royal was a social club for artists, a literary forum and a critical workshop for writers. Manuscripts and contracts often changed hands or were signed atop the marble tables.

Of the many stories about this café, the most famous may be of the fiery Marquess of Queensberry glowering across the room at the regular meetings of his son 'Bosie' Douglas and Oscar Wilde. When the Marquess lost his patience, Wilde wrote to his epicene young friend, 'Your father is on the rampage again – been to the Café Royal to inquire after us.' The lawsuit and trial of Wilde encouraged the press to portray the café as a den of sodomites. One day Frank Harris and George Bernard Shaw were dining when Wilde entered their private room for a frank discussion in

the course of which Harris told him he would 'lose his case for libel against Queensberry'. Had Wilde left for Paris, as advised, once his libel trial collapsed and before criminal proceedings against him began, the rest of his life would have been quite different.

Wilde's absence from London during his imprisonment and his subsequent final exile in France was keenly felt at the Café Royal. But the scandal did not discourage its literary habitués. Before the war the Bloomsbury Group, including Virginia Woolf, E. M. Forster and John Maynard Keynes, were regulars, as were the Sitwells, Marinetti and his Italian Futurists, his English admirer Wyndham Lewis, and the Vorticists.

Dylan Thomas confessed to having a 'peep' in to see if he could spot a 'literary great'. T. E. Hulme liked to sit in the café with critic Ashley Dukes.

Others were more caustic: D. H. Lawrence satirically described it as 'The Café Pompadour' in *Women in Love* (1921). Immediately after the Second World War, John Betjeman spotted the ageing Arthur Symons in the Royal, 'Very old and very grand'. During a later decade one journalist reports dining at the Royal and spotting among the throng Stephen Spender, Christopher Isherwood, Henry Moore, Sir Harold Nicolson and Sir Kenneth Clark.

The rich history of the Café Royal is chronicled in numerous books, paintings and memoirs. In 1954, hotelier Charles Forte took over the café and turned it into a showpiece of his gastronomic empire; several books marked the centenary in 1965. Café Royal is now owned by the French hotel group Le Meridien, whose London hotel is located nearby on Piccadilly.

ABOVE: The baroque Grill Room at Café Royal is one of the most glamorous and spectacular dining areas in the city. Cecil Beaton described it as 'the most beautiful room in London'. Its Victorian grandeur is displayed in ornate gilt-edge mirrors and hand-painted ceilings.

Kettners

29 ROMILLY STREET
SOHO
LONDON, ENGLAND

Other than the smart Café Royal, none of the old London coffee-houses have survived. Today writers work at home on their computers, or meet in pubs or clubs. Yet among what once were coffee-houses, Kettners survives because it has adapted to the needs of contemporary patrons. Founded in 1867 (not long after the Café Royal) by Auguste Kettner, the chef to Napoleon III, it shared with the Regent Street establishment its most famous patron, the Anglo-Irish dramatist Oscar Wilde; but the guest list included many other celebrities, including the playboy King Edward VII.

After going through several incarnations, Kettners was recently bought by Peter Boizot, founder of the Pizza Express group, who repainted and renovated the premises. It has kept its old colonial

OPPOSITE: Entrance to the three-storey Kettners Restaurant, founded in 1867 at the corner of Romilly and Greek streets in Soho, London's bohemian neighbourhood, near the theatre district.

RIGHT: The main dining room, its mirrors, painted walls and ceilings all carefully preserved, has windows out to both streets. The cosy bar and stuffed armchairs to the left of the entrance would still appeal to Oscar Wilde.

décor on three floors (someone called it 'three floors of posh decadence'). One can still see in the now refurbished architecture and interior what a grand place it was, even while all around it cool Britannia has become pub- and bar-centred.

Today, Kettners has a Champagne Bar, a wine bar, a piano room and eight private dining rooms. One can drink at the bar, sit down for pizza and champagne, or bring the family for Sunday lunch.

OPPOSITE: One of eight private dining rooms in Kettners, now available for private parties, with the original windows and wooden walls intact.

LEFT: Kettner's extensive wine cellar has been well stocked for a century and a half.

Heyday of the English Coffee-House

Addison at Buttons Coffee House c.1720

The coffee-house era in England lasted over a hundred years spanning the 17th and 18th centuries – a period also notable for a flowering of English literary achievement. Historians claim the coffee-houses helped nurture this blossoming of talent. At three o'clock every afternoon John Dryden held forth with his critical commentary in Will's Coffee-House at No. 1 Great Russell Street, where the standards he set in his discourse would explicate and elevate English literature for a century. About a dozen years after Dryden's death in 1700, Button's Coffee-House became headquarters for *The Spectator*, *The Guardian* and the *Tatler*, and for the men who wrote and read them, including Addison, Steele, Swift and Pope. Samuel Johnson and his Literary Club held forth at the Turk's Head, and Jonathan Swift at St James's Coffee-House. Particular groups were to be found in certain establishments: the French at Giles, Scots at Forest's; lawyers at Nando's or the Grecian, insurance agents at Garraway's, academics at Truby or Child's; Whigs at St James's and Tories at the Cocoa Tree; gamblers at White's, military men at Old Man's, merchants and bankers at Lloyd's. And a few coffee-houses were 'kept by Persons of that Sisterhood', according to *The Spectator*. Such a list implies both the centrality of the coffee-house to metropolitan society and the seeds of the exclusive men's clubs that were to emerge during the late 18th century, further stratifying English life. By the middle of the 19th century, tea, not coffee, had become the English national family drink, and Thomas Twining's coffee-house on The Strand turned exclusively to tea, forming the basis for his now world-famous tea company.

Café A Brasileira

RUA GARRETT 120–122
LISBON, PORTUGAL

Café A Brasileira, also called Brasileira do Chiado, is the most crowded and famous writers' café in this waterside capital. The life-size statue of the great poet Fernando Pessoa (1888–1935) dominates the terrace as a virtual icon. With its green-and-gold Art Nouveau façade, wooden chairs, brass railings, mirrored walls and long, oak-panelled bar, the café clearly comes from another era. Chandeliers illuminate the carved ceilings. Outside there are chairs under yellow umbrellas where patrons watch the crowds night and day. Café A Brasileira has been serving short, strong coffees and pastries since the 1920s. Though a devastating fire in 1988 destroyed many buildings in the area, the café has been restored in its former fashion.

Its location directly at a busy metro stop and near a university ensures that the café and its terrace are never empty. Tourists crowd the students for tables. The University of Lisbon's Faculdade de Belas-Artes has 1,300 students who enliven the quarter and pass here nearly every day on foot or in small electric trams. International newspapers and magazines are available just inside the café door.

The literati of Portugal made the Brasileira their chief meeting place. Pessoa, their greatest 20th-century poet, was a regular who enjoyed his absinthe and *bica* (espresso). He liked his coffee short, black and sweet, and he smoked continuously. Multilingual and multicultural, Pessoa wrote in both Portuguese and English. A giant in modern Portuguese culture, he published with his friends the review *Orpheus*.

The bronze statue of Pessoa statue in front of the café depicts him as a figure at a table with an empty bronze chair beside him, waiting – waiting for whom? Every tourist with a camera answers that question personally. One young Portuguese writer says: 'If we could melt the bronze Pessoa at his café table, he'd order another brandy, another coffee, light maybe his seventy-sixth cigarette of the day and, if he was comfortable, snap at the world with wit and dazzle us with his sharp mind. They say he was fun to be with.'

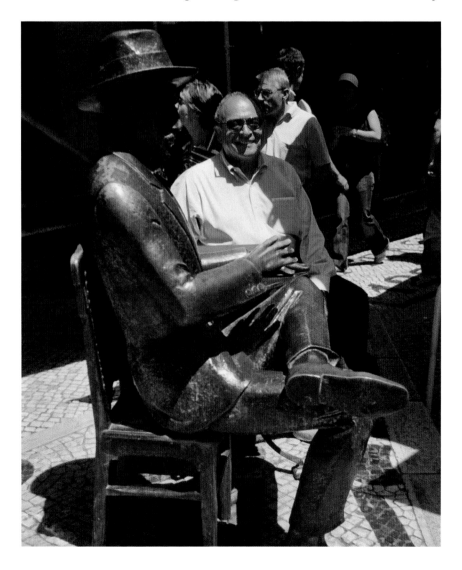

Pessoa is also commemorated in the cloister of the Jerónimos monastery by a marble pillar inscribed with verses he wrote under four pseudonyms. In 1985 his remains were entombed in this column in the cloister. A striking painting of him hangs in the Centre of Modern Art. One can find other paintings and photographs of him in this and other cafés and corners of Lisbon; but his statue as patron of the Café A Brasileira seems the most fitting memorial.

Pessoa wanted the world to know how great a city Lisbon was. He recreates it in mythic proportions, lamenting Portugal's destiny in his prophetic potent poetry: 'All is scattered, nothing entire. O Portugal, fog you are.' Like the Irish poet W. B. Yeats, he set up his own mythology and was influenced by the diabolist Aleister Crowley. He died aged only 47, but his complete manuscripts were not published until the 1980s. His books are all available in the large FNAC bookstore, just steps down the hill from the café.

LEFT: In warm weather, the dark wooden façade of the Brasileira is nearly obscured by the yellow awnings covering the outdoor tables.

OPPOSITE: Poet Fernando Pessoa, patron saint of Portuguese literature and of this café, keeps watch over the sidewalk patrons, welcoming Portuguese writers, neighbouring university students, and curious, camera-ready tourists who pose in the chair next to his statue.

Other Cafés in Portugal

The Lisbon café scene, which can be traced back to the 18th century and is influenced by that of Italy, had its greatest flowering between 1900 and 1930. Conté de Laxiadio once said that his country was ruled from its cafés. One of the oldest existing cafés (founded 1782) is Martinho da Arcada, originally Café Central, which was Pessoa's first café. The publicity postcard of the café, now called Café Restaurant Martinho da Arcada, is a photograph of Pessoa at a table there. On the walls are enlarged copies of his 1928 passport, his poetry, and a copy of José de Almorda Negeiros's 1913 illustration of Pessoa at his table. Literary debates and discussions continue even today, though the square is no longer the centre of the town except for trams and buses.

The Majestic Café, a national monument in Portugal's second city of Porto (Oporto) and its chief literary café, was immortalized by poet Antonio Ferro in 1922, a year after it was founded. A key figure in this city is Henry the Navigator, who seems to dominate its images (and even its language: to feed his sailors he took all produce from the city except its tripe, and the inhabitants even now call themselves 'the tripe-eaters'). The Majestic (112 Rua Santa Catarina) is in the grand style with a back patio, beyond the grand piano, and a terrace located on a pedestrian street. But it is the interior that draws the lingerers with its Art Nouveau décor of mirrors, gold trim, marble tabletops and carved ceilings dominated by smiling *putti* looking down at the writer working on his computer.

Every village in Portugal seems to have a coffee-house, most of them lined with the traditional decorative blue tile.

Café Comercial

GLORIETA DE BILBAO 7
MADRID, SPAIN

Founded on 26 December 1870, the Café Comercial is the oldest continuously operating café in Madrid. It was run by the Contreras family for most of the 20th century. The Comercial became an intellectual refuge during the long Franco era after some of the first anti-Franco protests in Spain began here. Even before that the café was popular with impoverished writers, and a bohemian air persists to this day. Then a café for the avant-garde, Republican aviators and artists, it now attracts young foreigners, whether artists or students.

The Café Comercial is located on a busy roundabout, infested by traffic but graced by a tall fountain at the Bilbao metro stop. Bookstalls surround the intersection and the café. The interior décor in a now somewhat shabby grand style includes marble stairs, floor tiles, pillars and huge mirrors. The square wooden tables are plain, and the rooms have clearly been harbouring coffee-drinkers and readers for more than a smoke-filled century. The Comercial has proudly resisted fashion and time.

'Spaniards are the most talkative creatures on earth. In our

LEFT: The main ground floor room of this treasured institution – described in the novels of several of its patrons – has a lofty chandeliered ceiling, heavy wooden tables, pillars, mirrored walls and a reputation for an intellectual atmosphere.

OPPOSITE: The usually busy entrance bar is curved to make a welcoming foyer for this typical city café owned by the same family since 1903. Eat *churros* (a doughnut-like pastry) with your coffee or take tapas with sherry.

into the internet – a perfect example of an old café adjusting to modern times. In the front room the dimensions are more intimate and the view across the plaza expansive. Here older men play chess and back-gammon under a circulating fan. A sign declares that anyone who sits down to play a game has to order a drink immediately.

Patrons of the Café Comercial have included film director Luis Berlanga and many writers of the 1960s and 1970s generations, among them Ignacio Aldecoa, Manuel Alcáctar and César González-Priano. More recent regulars include the architect and painter Rafael Escobedo Munoz, and Gerardo Diego. The menu lists a dozen famous patrons, including movie directors, actors (John Malkovich), performers (Celia Gámez), musicians (Munoz Román), bullfighters, politicians and university professors – a veritable pantheon of a century and more of the intellectual and artistic life of Madrid.

An excellent description of this café can be derived from a social portrait in Pérez Galdós's novel *Fortunata y Jacinta*, written in 1887: 'Full of people, the atmosphere was thick and suffocating, you could chew it, and there was a deafening noise like a beehive... Juan Pablo Ruvin didn't feel alive unless he spent half the day or almost all of it at a café.' Spain's Nobel Prize-winning novelist Camilo José Cela, in his 1953 novella *Café de Artistas*, portrays a revolving door swinging into the café, a stage for small-scale human drama. Today one enters the café via the large and busy bar, the gaze met by a coffee-maker, racks of newspapers, and a view to the left into the large sitting and meeting area where one can drink and read alone or meet a friend or friends for conversation.

ABOVE: On this busy street, overlooking Glorieta de Bilbao, most customers prefer the café inside, while the first floor (behind the balustrade) is chosen by the regulars who play chess and backgammon.

cafés anything under the sun is fair game for conversation,' said novelist Benito Pérez Galdós, who was the first to write about this café. The downstairs room still hosts traditional *tertulias* or discussion groups. Notices of forthcoming meetings are posted just inside the front door on the left. Stories from the *tertulias* are accessible in a more modern medium on the internet website www.margencero.com.

Up the marble stairway are smaller rooms. A back room handles the cyber-generation plugged

Café de Oriente

PLAZA DE ORIENTE 2
MADRID, SPAIN

The Café de Oriente, as elegant as the Café Comercial is shop-worn, was originally the monastery of the Franciscan order known as the 'Descalzos' (meaning 'bare-foot'), built by Felipe III in 1613. The present building is a beautiful, relatively recent (1982) but old-fashioned-looking café and restaurant, facing the Palacio Real (Royal Palace) and, further down to the left from the café terrace, the Almudena Cathedral. Next door to the right is the grey Royal Theatre and Opera House, whose patrons are drawn before and after the performances by the brilliantly lit and welcoming café. Together, the café and opera house dominate the crescent-shaped plaza that looks across its green park to the palace.

The Oriente, like the Café de la Paix in Paris, appeals today to an upmarket clientèle. The Spanish neo-Victorian furnishings remind one of Orient Express trains and historic ocean liners. Mighty and overpoweringly ornate chandeliers, expensive woods, a grand terrace and an artistic menu offering a variety of coffees make this perhaps the most impressive of Madrid's cafés.

Writers used to meet in the private salon beneath the café, a room with high brick ceiling arches that added drama to the privacy of their *tertulias*. Today this elegant cave serves as a positively rated restaurant, and

RIGHT: The graceful curved arcade, which also includes the Opera House next door, makes the elegant Café de Orient one of Europe's grandest. At the centre of the green plaza is an equestrian statue of King Philip IV designed by Velazquez (1599–1660).

OPPOSITE: Under the glass floor of the underground vault are pottery and artifacts unearthed during the construction of a Franciscan monastery on the site in 1613.

ABOVE: The second vaulted-ceiling cave beneath Café de Oriente is used as a dining room as well as a museum.

the *tertulias* are informal, friendly gatherings on the terrace in the summer or inside, accompanied by piano, on winter afternoons.

In 1924 the painter Salvador Dalí made an Indian ink drawing of Federíco García Lorca in the Café de Oriente. He signed, dated, and identified the subject of the painting. Another patron of Café de Oriente was a much admired bullfighter in whose commemoration García Lorca was to write his most famous poem, 'The Lament of Ignacio Sánchez Mejías'.

Occupying the corner of the building nearest the opera house is the café's *botilleria*, where the main feature is wine. The basement banqueting room, which can also be reached from the Oriente's downstairs restaurant, is a magnificent chamber with tables resting on a glass floor. It is virtually a museum, both archeologically and artistically. Visible beneath the floor are ancient ruins and dusty artefacts such as vases, remnants of the life over which the 1613 Franciscan monastery was built. On the walls one finds mementos as evidence of the café's public and private creative clientèle: drawings and signatures of past and present writers, actors and painters who have met here and in the room next door. Here is a veritable treasury of Old Madrid.

To get a similar feeling of underground caves and rich literary history, one should also visit Madrid's most famous literary restaurant (Hemingway praised its roast suckling pig): Restaurante Botin at Cuchilleros 17, founded in 1725.

Café de Gijón

PASEO DE RECOLETOS 21
MADRID, SPAIN

Madrid's archetypal literary café is the Gijón, known for its role as a meeting place of intellectuals. The café kept alive the tradition of the 18th-century *tertulia*, a festive but informal discussion group. Madrid has long summers, so one finds many open terrace cafés: the pavement terrace of the Gijón, typical of this capital city's coffee-house tradition and climate, spills onto the small pedestrianized area between two streets.

Just inside the door is a local character, Señor Alfonso, who sells cigarettes, international magazines and newspapers (and the history of the café). Once inside you see the red burn-stained banquettes that betray a century of use. Saturated with history and culture and tobacco, the café's robust simplicity fascinates the newcomer. Don 'Pepe' José Lopez de Brito, the coffee-house count of Madrid, has for many years stood behind the bar talking to customers and presiding over the Gijón. He and his sister, Marissa, are the third generation of owners of this last

bastion of the tradition of grand cafés in Madrid.

Situated on the very Madrilenian promenade, Paseo de Recoletos, an upmarket area of ministries and banks, Gijón was founded by an Asturian named Don Gumersindo Gomez in 1888. In 1913 it was sold on the condition that it continue as a café with the same name, a name that had brought honor to the city of Gijón (as well as to Madrid). Some historians date its founding to 1916, the year it reopened under new management.

The first glory days of the Gijón stretched from the end of the 19th century through to the early 1930s – a period called the grand 'Madrilenian Bohemian' period. During this time, two generations of writers met and kept the *tertulias* alive.

The first was the *fin de siécle* group, whose patrons included Rubén Darío, the early 20th-century Latin American modernist poet, and Pablo Neruda, one of Latin America's most famous 20th-century poets and essayists. The second was called the Generation of '98, a group that included Azorín (pseudonym for novelist José Martínez Ruiz), the novelist Pío Barója and the poet Antonio Machado. Also prominent was Ramón del Valle Inclán, a famous dramatist, known for his *esperpento* style of writing in which he distorts reality like a concave mirror to present a caricature of Spanish society. Valle Inclán is probably the most characteristic literary figure connected to the Gijón, for he was the embodiment of the café writer.

Other illustrious Gijón patrons included the novelists Benito Pérez Galdós and Camilo José Cela (famous for the *tremendista* style of writing). In Cela's 1951 novel *La Colmena* (The Hive), the action revolves around a café, which he portrays as a microcosm of Madrid society. Another regular

ABOVE: Surly waiters, black-and-white marble tables, and square-tiled floors characterize Madrid's best known café, founded in 1916. The Gijón remained open throughout the Spanish Civil War (1936–9), when its patrons included supporters of Franco, and then, later, the intellectual opposition.

OPPOSITE: The wood-lined basement is now called the museum because self-caricatures and poems by the artistic clientèle line its walls.

ABOVE: A wide selection of wines await customers amid the museum memorabilia.

RIGHT: Spanish Surrealist painter Salvador Dalí (1904-1989) was a patron who sketched in cafés, leaving his own image for the café's wall.

visitor was Federíco García Lorca (of the 'Generation of '27'), the most important Spanish dramatist of the 20th century (*Blood Wedding*), who was executed early in the Spanish Civil War.

Other Gijón patrons included dramatist Fernando Arrabál and film-maker Luis Buñuel, along with Salvador Dalí and Ernest Hemingway, who was in Spain along with many writers, soldiers and journalists covering the civil war. Hemingway found the clientèle snobbish. Today he might be offended by the grumpy waiters.

The Gijón enjoyed a period of renewed splendour between 1940 and 1960. By then, under Franco, many of the other traditional cafés had disappeared or changed their function because they had become unprofitable (too many people sitting for hours over one cup of coffee). After the Civil War, intellectuals came for social gatherings at the Gijón, more animated by the artistic discussions than by politics. Theatre openings, other cultural events and late suppers brought a diverse crowd here, as well as to the nearby grand café of the Theatre of Fine Arts (Teatro de Bellas Artes).

Fortunately, after a time of instability in which it

was rumoured that it might disappear, the Gijón continues to thrive today, its doors still open after more than 100 years. El Museo del Gran Café Gijón downstairs has long tables for discussion groups, vaulted wooden ceilings and walls covered with memorabilia. Instead of the usual photographs signed by celebrity artists, they have self-portait drawings, poetry and personal words praising the café. One writer begins by quoting Portugal's poet Pessoa and ends by suggesting: 'Let's replace degustation with fornication.'

'It was late and every one had left the [Madrid] café except an old man who sat in the shadow the leaves of the tree made against the electric light. In the day time the street was dusty, but at night the dew settled the dust and the old man liked to sit late because he was deaf and now at night it was quiet and he felt the difference.'

ERNEST HEMINGWAY,
'A CLEAN, WELL-LIGHTED PLACE'

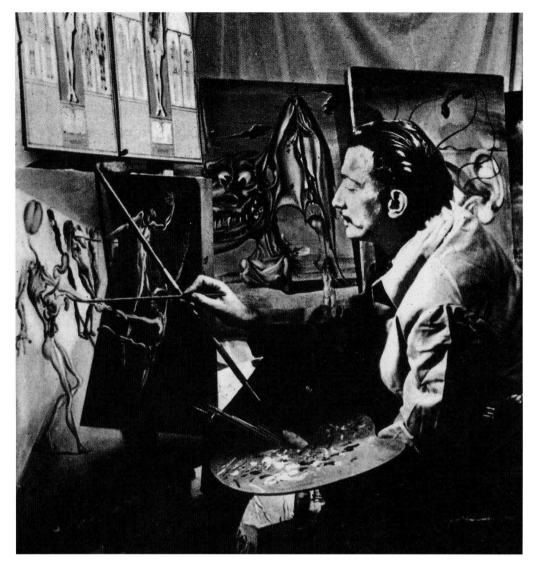

Café Pombo, Madrid

One of the important Spanish cafés in the early 20th century was Madrid's Café Pombo (1912–1925), which shared many customers with the Gijón. These two cafés carried on the centuries-old tradition of the *tertulia*, the gathering to discuss literature or philosophy. One historian describes the early cafés as cultural caves of conspirators like those of ancient Athens: caves for leaders of the arts, intellectual life, public policy and culture (including the bullfighters). Mariano José de Larra was a pioneer of Spanish journalism and a hero of café society. One of the most important groups to meet here gathered around Ramón Gómez de la Serna (1888–1963), a student of Valle-Inclán. Here, in the café's cellar (called the 'Cripta de Pombo'), Serna created the *Greguería* style, which became an indispensable part of Spanish lyric writing, mixing aphorism, humour and prose poetry. His two-volume *Pombo* was written in 1918, and he wrote many other books about Spain's cafés. He declared that Café Pombo was 'so unique it was like Jesus' tomb'.

Café Els Quatre Gats

MONTSIÓ 3 BIS
BARCELONA, SPAIN

It was here in 1900 that the 16-year-old Pablo Picasso presented his art to the world for the first time. The prodigy was a part of a group of Catalan painters who met in the café regularly and were an important Iberian branch of the École de Paris art movement. The interaction between these painters and the Parisian trends helped create Modernism. Indeed, the Catalan painters of this generation have come to be called the 'Els Quatre Gats group' in Spanish art history, for the café and these artists emerged just as Barcelona was becoming a modern industrial and commercial centre.

Café Els Quatre Gats (The Four Cats) opened noisily with much fanfare on 12 June 1897. In charge of the café was Père Romeu, who, among several professions, had been a cabaret waiter in Paris's Chat Noir (Black Cat) cabaret. His partners in the venture were Manuel Girona, president of Barcelona's chamber of commerce, and Ramon Casas. Other businessmen contributed to the financing, and Santiago Russiñyol created the original poster. The announcement of its opening heralded the Quatre Gats as a place 'for those people of good taste' who need earthly nourishment as well as 'nourishment of the mind'.

LEFT: A narrow alleyway (*carrer*) leads to this brick-faced Gothic revival café, one of the most unusual and lively of Europe's café landmarks, frequented by some of the most famous names in Spain's artistic past.

OPPOSITE: Els Quatre Gats has traditional Catalan arches, tiles, and art on the walls informing visitors of the café's background as a centre for artists since the turn of the 20th century. Customers still sometimes gather around the piano to sing.

ABOVE: In the front room of the colorful 4Gats, lined with tiles, are photographs of its founders and artistic patrons (Picasso, Miró, Utrillo, Gaudi) as well as the Ramon Casas's bicycle placard (used as a café logo).

'This will be an inn for those who have lost their appetite, a warm corner for those who miss their home, a museum for those who seek to taste delicacies for the soul, a tavern and a trellis for those who like the shade of grape arbors and the juice of the grape; it is a gothic brasserie for the lovers of the north and an Andalou patio for lovers of the south; it is a presbytery, a church yard for the sick of our century, a centre of friendship and harmony for those who come to rest within its doors.'

The café was built in a Neo-Gothic house that had just been constructed at the corner of a little square. The end of the long café was easily converted into an exhibition hall. The name Els Quatre Gats was certainly intended to be an echo of or tribute to The Black Cat in Paris, for Romeu tried to recreate here the atmosphere of Montmartre. The walls were covered with paintings. Picasso was a regular by 1899, and in 1900, the year of his first public exhibition, he drew another '4Gats' image or poster that is prominently featured today.

The cabaret closed on 19 July 1903 and, though a group continued to meet there until 1936, the building fell into disrepair. When it was reopened in the 1970s as 4Gats, the newspaper articles marking the event (framed on the wall today) featured Picasso and his proud Catalonian origins. Fully restored by 1989, the large, dark building still features ground-floor glass arcades. Upstairs, the wooden gallery runs around the dining area and is also used for drinking and dining. There is live piano music and patrons often sing along.

In the café's beautiful tiled bar area, which is the front room reserved for drinking, stands a shiny coffee machine with the café's logo on it. Since 1995 the café holds regular literary meetings and has been publishing a journal. After the centenary in 1997, an enormous new painting of two men on a bicycle built for two was hung in the bar area, where every corner and wall space is covered with carvings, plates, bottles and framed pictures, most notably one of the founder, Père Romeu.

Café de l'Ópera

LA RAMBLA DELS CAPUTXINS 74
BARCELONA, SPAIN

Opened as a restaurant in 1876 for the elite of Barcelona, today these premises belong to everyone, especially visitors to the opera and the talented artists who perform there. Tenor Alfredo Kraus signed the guest book here in 1992, and Placido Domingo visited on 8 February 2005. Verdi opera posters line the walls of the room upstairs, whose windows look directly across the Rambla to the Liceu Theatre.

This popular two-storied café, now called Café de l'Ópera, is an international meeting point, with an afterglow of the golden days. For Spain and Catalonia alike it is a part of both national and regional history. King Alfonso XIII, anarchists, politicians, union leaders, writers, bohemians, musicians and intellectuals have all passed through here. Three books of signatures and hundreds of anecdotes are inscribed in the *livre d'or*. Fernando Rey, the Spanish actor famed for his performances in Buñuel's films, added his signature in 1993.

If Madrid, with its monumental buildings, is Spain's cosmopolitan metropolis, Barcelona by the sea has its own international flair. A busy port and industrial centre, it is also a vacation spa, often full of swarms of holidaymakers, who fill every seat on the Ramblas on warm nights. Serious café visitors come inside for the comfortable green and ochre colours and the lively café action. Recent celebrities include famous touring athletes such as Charles Barkley (under whose signature in the guest book, on 28 July 1992, the management added 'Jugudor NBA'). The President of the Parliament of Catalonia signed the guest book in 1995.

Barcelona is the capital of the region of Catalonia, and its population prides itself on speaking Catalan (a language long banned by Franco) as well as Spanish and French. The three greatest Catalonian

RIGHT: From the entrance to this lovely little jewel box of a café one can see the pastry cases that tempted painters, like Miró, and opera singers, including Placido Domingo. Walls of the upstairs room are covered with posters of female opera figures.

painters – Picasso, Miró, Dalí – were patrons of Café de l'Opera and proudly Catalan. Barcelona's cafés are a reflection of the often playful Catalan lifestyle and culture, as are the Gaudí architecture of many buildings, the Mies Van der Rohe lines of pavement benches (from his famous 'Barcelona chair') and the tomato bread.

The café enjoys a key location, across from the Liceu opera house and metro stop of the same name, on on La Rambla – the most famous street in Barcelona (and one of the most frequented pedestrian streets in Europe). From an Arabic word meaning 'torrent', La Rambla follows the course of a former seasonal riverbed (a road in dry weather) and is the city's promenade for citizens and tourists (the 'paseo' is a nightly ritual). Trees were planted in the 16th century, and by the 18th century the bourgeoisie had taken over from the religious orders (including the Caputxins Monastery), building their opulent palaces. In the 19th century La Rambla was lined with elegant bank buildings and flower shops. Today the flowers are sold in stalls that alternate with clusters of café tables that line the wide walkway.

The Café de l'Ópera is on a portion of the street called Rambla dels Caputxins, constructed next to the second wall (destroyed) of the 13th-century medieval city. The building, one of the few reminders of an earlier age, was at first a restaurant and hotel for the carriage trade leaving the city for Madrid. With the arrival of the opera house (Gran Teatre del Liceu, 1837–48), it became an elegant chocolate shop with paintings of the

royal court on the walls. In 1890 it converted to an aristocratic café and restaurant called La Mallorquina with traditional painted walls, only to be transformed yet again in 1928 into a Modernist style (the Modernista movement was a Catalan phenomenon).

Since its inauguration in 1929, the Café de l'Opera has not stopped serving, even during the tumultuous Spanish Civil War. Only recently was the café, with its chandeliers, marble steps and mirrors, restored once more by the architect Antoni Moragas to be preserved as a national treasure. The green-and-ochre-stained walls and ceilings of this narrow café and the non-stop arrival of its patrons make this a crowded and welcome treasure.

Caffè Pedrocchi

VIA VIII FEBBRAIO 15
PADUA, ITALY

Called by many the oldest continously operating café in Europe, the Pedrocchi is certainly the grandest. The citizens of Padua had already begun drinking coffee in 1683. By 1756 there were 206 cafés, but no one had seen the likes of what was to become the Café Pedrocchi. The original café on this site opened in 1760; the present one, built (after the destruction of the first) was constructed between 1815 and 1831. Antonio Pedrocchi intended his coffee-house to be the most beautiful in Europe, one for artists and 'high flyers'. He succeeded.

The Pedrocchi is located in the centre of the city, close by the university, and students have always been among its patrons. But it was the enthusiasm of architects, artists and in particular the great French Italophile Stendhal

RIGHT: The neo-Gothic 'Pedrocchio' (once a pastry shop) on the left next door is joined (at the upper floor) to the south façade of the Pedrocchi. A single loggia graces this side of the café. The top floor is now a museum. This is the most ambitiously designed café in Europe and drew admiring architects as well as such illustrious writers as Stendhal, George Sand, Théophile Gautier, and Gabriele D'Annunzio.

OPPOSITE: A through-view of the ground-floor, looking from the north loggia into the bar, called the Green Room, where newspapers await the morning coffee drinkers. One can look through two other café rooms to the street beyond. Doors on all three sides are glass and open directly onto three streets or piazzas. Hence, it is called 'the café without doors'.

ABOVE: The Red Room, in the shape of a basilica, features a curved bar. On the floor above the café are twelve rooms, each decorated by a great artist illustrating a period of Padua's history – a great museum (with an admission fee that is well worth the price).

('l'excellent restaurateur Pedrocchi, le meilleur d'Italie et presque égal à ceux de Paris'). 'It was in Padua', he went on, 'that I began to see life in the Venetian way, women in the cafés in society festively meeting until two in the morning.'

Architects and critics agree with the novelist that this was a building to rival the splendours of Paris and London, with its façade of massive columns, a grand balcony sustained by Doric pillars, and two stone lions at the base of a marble staircase leading to the majestic entryway. No wonder the café was called a temple and was frequented by such illustrious foreign writers as Théophile Gautier, the Goncourt brothers and Maxim Gorky.

Designed by the prestigious Venetian architect Giuseppe Japelli, who also designed the Art School of Padua, the café radiates a sense of permanence and historical importance befitting a cathedral or museum. The exterior is Greek, and the many doors are completely glass, which when open transform the place into a 'café without doors'. The interior is a mixture of styles, with rooms for billiards, reading and dining. Architects see it as a major example of Italian Neo-classicism. Leopoldo Cicognara, diplomat and academician, called it 'one of the most successfully imagined and artfully constructed [cafés] in Europe… unusual, superb and unexpected… a masterpiece… a sumptuous palace'. Gautier had the same kind of experience: 'nothing is more monumentally classical… the ensemble very grand'. The critic Pierre Selvatico said with all its grandeur it did 'not lose its conviviality', praise that must have pleased Pedrocchi.

The first floor above, now the Museo del Risorgimento e dell'Età Contemporanea (Museum of the Risorgimento and of the Contemporary Age), 'presents a history of interior decoration through the ages'. At the top of the marble stairs, one enters the Etruscan Room with its four semi-elliptical columns, followed by the many-sided Greek Room,

which drew all the great writers from Europe past its portals.

In 1831 the new Pedrocchi made its luxurious début at the celebration of the 600th anniversary of the death of St Anthony of Padua. The finished work is a more or less triangular building of marble and crystal, containing geographical paintings, many lamps, elegant tables and walls decorated by a variety of artists. The high, contrasting Neo-Gothic façade of the wing next to the café was opened in 1836 and called 'Il Pedrocchino'. It became the pastry shop.

At the beginning of his great novel *The Charterhouse of Parma*, Stendhal called the café 'the best in Italy and almost the equal of those in Paris'

ABOVE: Gabriele D'Annunzio (1863-1938), Italian poet, novelist, and dramatist, visited this café and the Greco in Rome.

RIGHT: The charming curved bar of the Red Room serves, for those who wish to stand, coffee and champagne with elegant pastries.

with frescos and doors to the other period rooms: the circular jewel of a Roman Room, decorated with images of Rome; the Baroque Room; the Renaissance Room, with carved ceiling and blue tapestry walls; the Herculean Room; the Egyptian Room; and the tiny Moorish Room, with smoked mirrors, birds, and plants decorating the walls. Near the back loggia are the Greek Room, with coats of arms painted on the window, and the Fencing Room, now the museum of the history of Padua after the downfall of the Republic of Venice. Finally comes the grandest: the Rossini Room, honouring the Italian opera composer and bon vivant, a room many thought the most beautiful of all, and one still used for public events.

On the ground floor, the café's many rooms include a newspaper room, two front terraces and the Red Room, with its grand piano and elegant curved bar. The White Room illustrates the revolt against the Austrians in 1848. During the building's construction, ancient ruins were discovered. Once incorporated into the design of the café at a level beneath the entry under a glass floor, they have now been moved to a museum.

Such was the fame of this majestic café that in 1845 Padua even witnessed the birth of a newspaper called *Caffè Pedrocchi*. As the French social historian Lemaire says, writers came from all over the world to establish in literature the myth of this café.

Caffè Florian

PIAZZA SAN MARCO 56–59
VENICE, ITALY

From Casanova to Lord Byron, Goethe to Proust, James Joyce to Gertrude Stein, everyone seems to have frequented the Florian, listened to the orchestra and watched the throngs in Venice's Piazza San Marco. Many artists, including Bertini and Canaletto, have painted this café. Like the Quadri across the Piazza, Caffè Florian is famous for its large terrace (holding up to 200 chairs) and for its orchestra. Inside, the mirrored little rooms are glorious. Of all the cafés in this 1,500-year-old city, this is the undisputed queen.

The Florian was founded in 1720 as 'Venice Triumphant', but renamed after its first proprietor, Floriano Francesconi. The walls are covered with paintings showing crowds of Venetians gathered outside under the arcade and on the piazza fronting the Florian. In 1848, when the long Austrian occupation was temporarily brought to an end, the owner wanted to transform his café into a dazzling display. He hired the artist Ludovico Cadorin, and ten years later his café reopened on 24 July 1858. Numerous rooms became like little candy boxes, with allegorical paintings on the walls and framed mirrors, in what

LEFT: Under the arcade at night, one can see each of the six elegant coffee rooms.

RIGHT: From the Piazza San Marco, the Caffè Florian, with its famous orchestra, has been a Venice institution for almost 300 years. Founded in 1720 and named after its first proprietor, its present décor dates from the 19th century. In its heyday it was the venue of elegant Venetian and international society, which included Goldoni, Casanova, Rousseau, Byron, Goethe, Alfred de Musset and George Sand.

has been called the Pompadour style. Red velvet sofas lined the walls, tables were covered with marble, and even the walnut floor was decorated. Six of these rooms look out on the piazza. Leaders of Venice attended the gala opening, including Antonio Selva, architect of La Fenice opera house. The Florian soon became known as Il Salotto del Senato, 'the Living Room of the Senate'.

Novelist William Dean Howells, President Lincoln's Consul in Venice from 1861 to 1865, observed that the Austrians and Italians carefully chose their separate cafés, and yet the Florian 'seems to be the only common ground in the city on which the hostile forces consent to meet'. Howells

ordered an ice-cream there, as does the narrator of *The Aspern Papers*, in which Henry James describes 'how the immense cluster of tables and little chairs stretches like a promontory into the smooth lake of the Piazza. The whole place, of a summer's evening, under the stars and with all the lamps… is like an open-air saloon dedicated to cooling drinks and to a still finer degustation – that of the exquisite impressions received during the day.'

Throughout the centuries, the Florian has been a meeting place for the leaders of all the arts. Italian playwright Carlo Goldoni (1707–93) was a regular, as was sculptor Antonio Canova (1757–1822). Stendhal learned here of the defeat of Napoleon at Waterloo. Wagner chose the upper floor to listen to his music being played below. Madame Récamier, Chateaubriand, Alfred de Musset, George Sand and the Goncourt brothers visited from France; Charles Dickens, John Ruskin and Robert Browning from England. D. H. Lawrence, who was less enchanted, called Venice 'an abhorrent, green, slippery city'. The Caffè Florian appears in numerous films and fiction, including Henry James's *Roderick Hudson* as well as *The Aspern Papers*. In his *Further Reminiscences* (1889), English novelist Anthony Trollope records his 1871 impressions of the 'very small rooms, almost to be called cells, each corresponding with one arch of the arcade which lines the side of the Piazza'. Trollope found the café open at three and four in the morning and took a 'very comfortable breakfast' of eggs to accompany his bread and coffee.

The Florian and the Quadri, with their ground-floor coffee-rooms, great terraces and large competing orchestras, became places of pilgrimage. On hot afternoons, the white curtains hanging between the arches protect the clientèle from the sun; on windy, cold days, they warm the ambience. Intimate lights illuminate the night.

Music-lovers visiting Venice in the 21st century now report that the orchestras at the two cafés have

improved immensely because of the influx of East European musicians. A 5 euro 'music supplement' is added to your bill.

The 14 million tourists who visit Venice every year are a far cry from the wealthy and élite café-society patrons of yesteryear. Even the residents of Venice now number only half what they were in 1960. As a self-supporting city, Venice remains in decline, populated now by tourists who congregate en masse in Piazza San Marco.

Around the corner from the Florian and not to be missed is Gran Caffè Chioggia (San Marco 8), with the best view of the palace, clock tower and canal. Thomas Mann's hero in *Death in Venice* chose this café on the Piazzetta as his favourite.

ABOVE: Beneath each wide arch is framed one jewelbox room with marble tables, gilt-framed pictures, and Murano glassware. This one has access to the floors above and serves as a shop.

OPPOSITE: To enter any one of the little coffee rooms is to step back in time to the mid-19th century when the café was last fully refurbished.

Caffè Quadri

PIAZZA SAN MARCO 120–124
VENICE, ITALY

The Florian's eternal rival is Caffè Quadri, which was founded about 1775, 55 years after the Florian opened. Their orchestras play in competition or in tandem. Equal opportunity pigeons clutter the air and befoul the walkways between the tables outdoors, taking flight when the bells of the Campanile toll. Day-trippers wander by each café with their cameras, contemplating the exorbitant cost of a coffee on the terrace. Yet only at the Quadri, on the north side of Piazza San Marco, can one catch the morning sun and enjoy a view across the piazza to the Laguna.

In its early years, when Giorgio Quadri from Corfu was owner, this and a few other Venetian cafés were characterized by gambling, vice and hired rooms 'for purposes of debauch', in accordance with the city's historical reputation for accommodating sex. Even a hundred years later, when English writers Anthony Trollope and

John Ruskin patronized the Quadri, John Murray in his *Handbook for Travellers in Northern Italy* says that the flower girls were 'permitted to be important'.

Historically, the major contrast between the Quadri and the Florian emerged during the long Austrian occupation of Venice, when the Austrians chose the Quadri as their café while, logically, the patriotic locals chose the opposite side of the square.

The German composer Richard Wagner is said to have worked on *Tristan und Isolde* at the tables here. More than likely he worked on it in his head, for his routine after he arrived in Venice in 1858, according to his *Autobiography*, was to work on his opera until 2pm before taking a gondola to the Piazza for lunch. Here he listened to the military bands playing, and was sometimes 'startled… by the sound of my own overtures.' No one applauded, he noted, for the bands were the occupying Austrian military bands, whom he visited one day in the barracks where they rehearsed. He reveals in the autobiography that the long note of the horn in the beginning of the third act of *Tristan* is probably the echo of a gondolier cry he heard on the Grand Canal: 'a rough lament [was answered, and] this melancholy dialogue… affected me so much that I could fix the very simple musical component parts in my memory'.

The Quadri's owner in the mid-19th century, when Austrian rule ended and the Florian closed and transformed itself, did not want to seem less regal than his rival, so he hired the Florian's architect to oversee the renovation, redecoration and painting of tableaux on the Quadri walls.

After arriving in Venice from London in February 1881 with his novel *The Portrait of a Lady* nearly completed, Henry James took his lunch here every day (breakfast was at the Florian). He had been in the city before, in 1872, when it was

less crowded. Now, in his view, Venice had unfortunately been 'improved'. Reconstruction was going on in the Cathedral, and the vaporetto had been introduced to the Grand Canal. In one of his essays in *Italian Hours*, James remarks on the 'horde of savage Germans encamped in the Piazza… The English and Americans came a little later… with a great many French, who were discreet enough to make very long repasts at the Caffè Quadri, during which they were out of the way.' One wonders what

ABOVE: In one of only two small rooms that remain on the ground floor, John Ruskin and the last generation of 19th-century writers ate and drank.

OPPOSITE: Richard Wagner and Henry James admired the beautiful night view of the Quadri and its orchestra music.

he would say about the 21st-century tourists who 'infest' (to use James's word) the piazza today.

Certainly, in the warm months the Quadri seems to be taken over by tourists. But 'tourist Venice *is* Venice,' insists American writer Mary McCarthy in *Venice Observed*: 'the gondolas, the sunsets, the changing light, Florian's, Quadri's, Torcello, Harry's Bar, Murano, Burano, the pigeons, the glass beads, the vaporetto. Venice is a folding picture-post-card of itself.' Like Proust, James and Hemingway, McCarthy found Venice irresistible and difficult to leave.

As in all Italian cafés as from 2005, there is no smoking indoors at the Quadri, where the number of rooms has diminished since the 19th century. Only two rooms are left on the ground floor (others have been given over to commercial shops), and upstairs, where Byron, Alexandre Dumas and Marcel Proust used to dine, only two restaurant rooms, recently renovated, remain.

Giubbe Rosse

PIAZZA DELLA REPUBBLICA
13/14R
FLORENCE, ITALY

This grand old café was long a meeting place for the Florentine intellectual community, especially during the period prior to the First World War. Described in a novel by Aldo Palazzeschi (1988) as 'resembling a German beer hall in the middle of a Tuscan capital', it was originally an antique wine shop in what was then called Piazza Vittorio Emmanuele II. It later became a drinking establishment called Reninghaus, named for the two German brothers, brewers, who founded it in the mid-19th century as a meeting place for Florence's German community. In 1881 it became the Gran Caffè Ristorante Giubbe Rosse and dressed the waiters in red coats.

Italy's most eminent writers gathered here: F. T. Marinetti, Italo Svevo, Alberto Moravia, Umberto Saba. The French writer Valéry Larbaud was also a regular when in Florence. Moravia writes that at the time the 'real capital of Italian literature was Florence'. A large framed collage of the faces of these 'Artisti e Letterati' hangs on the wall facing the cashier. Individual paintings and drawings of and by famous patrons cover the surrounding walls.

In 1909 Marinetti's Futurists published their provocative manifesto, arousing great controversy. They were attacked by another Florentine group called 'La Voce', named after the magazine published by Prezzolini. Marinetti, Boccioni, Russolo and Carlo Carrà immediately went to Giubbe Rosse from Milan to confront Soffici, the author of the article, in the café. First there were fisticuffs; then tables flew amid much yelling and screaming. Eventually the Futurist and Vocianist artistic movements agreed that their goals were similar, so peace was made in the third room of the Giubbe Rosse. These young artists and writers eventually worked together against the literary establishment, and this café became their headquarters.

The Futurists wanted to shock the prevailing institutionalized Romanticism by celebrating the aesthetics of warfare and the machine. Pictures of these Futurists dominate the faces on the walls near the large curved bar in the first room.

When Café Paszkoski (1896) came to life across the street, between 1909 and 1913, the writers of Florence made this café another centre of intellectual life. (It is still a 'café concerto',

with grand piano, and has excellent historical pictures on the wall.) Dozens of writers involved in two literary journals, *Voce* and *Lacerba*, went back and forth between the cafés every night for years. Alberto Viviani, the historian of the Giubbe Rosse, says the 'liveliest minds of Italy' exchanged theories here, creating controversies and initiating new works: Polazzeschi, Papini, Amendola, Slataper and De Robertis are a few of the names he lists. Viviani believes 'it was like [Paris's] Closerie des Lilas on the grand occasions there . . . a veritable orgy of poetry and intelligence'.

In 1910 the Giubbe Rosse was renovated in Art Nouveau style, though the waiters retained their red coats. While some historians say its golden age ended in 1918, a new and even younger group formed here in the 1920s, founding *Solaria*, a magazine that played an important role in Florentine art by refusing any political involvement (their weapon was silence). The poet Eugenio Montale's hermeticism influenced their attitude towards European culture. Prominent devotees of this period make up another roll of honour: Montale, Italo Svevo, Umberto Saba, Valery Larbaud, André Gide, Gordon Craig, as well as other French and Italians of note.

Closed during the American occupation after the

ABOVE: During the summer months this wide outside terrace is busy with customers for morning espresso and afternoon drinks.

OPPOSITE: The long bar of the house of red coats, where the walls are covered with memorabilia and images of the Futurists who met and organized here.

Second World War, the Giubbe Rosse reopened in 1947. Today the walls are covered with artwork and the café spills out into the piazza, now called Piazza della Repubblica. The change of name had occurred shortly after Italian unification, in 1895, when the government, in an attempt to redeem what it considered the 'squalor' of the ancient city centre, built the triumphant Roman-style arches to enclose the piazza.

The Caffè Storico Letterario Giubbe Rosse is a cultural and preservation foundation that sponsors discussion groups at the café and announces them by flyer on the table inside. Their new postcard features pictures of recent wars with the assertion 'No war is ever holy,' an echo of the Solaria group's stand in the 1920s. Historians, according to the foundation, look back to the café's great history and hear the echo: 'César-Auguste-Octave: café, cappucino, absinth.'

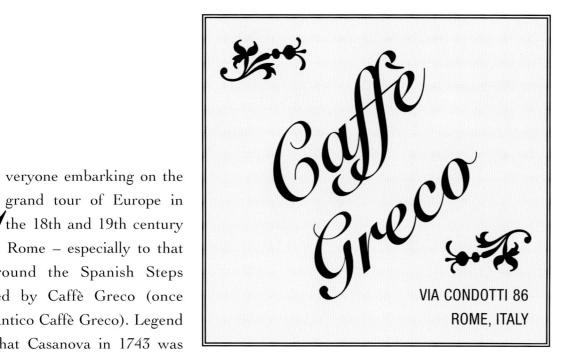

Caffè Greco

VIA CONDOTTI 86
ROME, ITALY

Everyone embarking on the grand tour of Europe in the 18th and 19th century went to Rome – especially to that area around the Spanish Steps anchored by Caffè Greco (once called Antico Caffè Greco). Legend has it that Casanova in 1743 was among the first patrons of the Greco, and that an assignation he had hoped for was frustrated by a woman there. But, sweet as that legend may be, the café was not founded until 1760. If one glances today at the portrait medallions of Liszt, Wagner, Gogol, the Prince of Bavaria and others on the walls and finds the little bronze statue of Mark Twain, one comes away with some sense of the international importance of this café. Like the Giubbe Rosse in Florence, it was a factory of literature; from the little back rooms emerged

numerous new ideas and artistic movements.

Artists, particularly the 'École de Rome', made this café their own in the 19th century. The Nazarenes were a group of German-speaking Romantic artists who had come from Vienna about 1809 (Cornelius, Riedel, Schwinde, Joseph Wagner), so named because they wore their hair long and flowing, *alla nazarena*. In addition to anonymous art students from around the world, patrons included two celebrated sculptors, Antonio Canova and the Swede Bertel Thorvaldsen. A group of early photographers from France, England and Italy gathered here in the 1840s, and were called the Caffè Greco Group. Chief among this group were Frédéric Flachéron, Eugène Constant, Alfred-Nicolas Norman, James Andersen and Giacomo Canova.

The English, who once haunted the now-defunct English Coffee House around the corner in Piazza di Spagna, soon came to prefer the Greco, among them Lord Byron and Percy Bysshe Shelley. William Makepeace Thackeray went to Rome to celebrate soon after publishing his novel *Vanity Fair*, and for a while lived near the Greco. Keats spent the last three months of his life here and died in a small room on the third floor of a building to the right of the Spanish Steps. 'Go thou to Rome, at once the Paradise,' wrote Shelley in his tribute to Keats. Shelley is buried, as is Keats, in the Protestant Cemetery in Rome, where Oscar Wilde wrote his poem 'The Grave of Shelley'.

As the English drifted away from the Greco, it

OPPOSITE: The modest entrance to one of Europe's oldest and most venerable cafés, patronized by Goethe, Schopenhauer, Byron, Shelley, Wagner, Stendhal, Thackeray, Gogol, and Twain (whose figure stands in a small alcove within the café), to name but a few.

RIGHT: The inescapable glass-encased pastry and sandwich display entices the visitor just inside the door.

improvised a public celebration with torches to honour him. Caffè Greco remained for some time the *rendez-vous des Allemands* (the meeting place of the Germans), attracting Goethe, Schopenhauer and Nietzsche. Wilhelm Müller, the poet, expressed his discontent with the regular patrons of Greco as 'men with arrogant manners'. Later, Felix Mendelssohn complained, in a vivid account in his *Letters from Italy and Switzerland* (1830), of the 'small dark room, about eight yards square', big dogs, hairy faces, 'fearful clouds of smoke' and the cursing of this German congregation not to be admired! When many of the German artists moved to the Caffè Colonna about 1860, they called their association the 'Colonna-Gesellschaft' (Colonna Association).

Nikolai Gogol, the great Russian master of prose, wrote some of his picaresque novel *Dead Souls* (1845) here, while dreaming of his native country. Visiting musicians included Franz Liszt, Richard Wagner and Felix Mendelssohn. Among notable American visitors were Nathaniel Hawthorne and Mark Twain. Other visiting literary luminaries came from France: Charles Baudelaire, Anatole France, Hippolyte Taine, Stendhal – and prix de Rome composer Hector Berlioz, who described the world-famous café as 'a ghastly tavern' of wooden benches and tables. It was not the austere décor, with its black (in fact marble) tables, but the company that drew so many writers, artists and composers.

In *Europe without Baedeker* (1947) the American literary critic Edmund Wilson remembers his impressions of the Greco after the Second World War. The café was still dim and dingy, and it was already trading on its heritage: 'If you hint of a tip, the waiter… will show you the yellow old albums in which the great men have signed their names.' Needless to say, the interior has been remodelled many times over the centuries, but the portrait medallions still grace the walls.

became the meeting place of the Germans, who constituted the majority of its clientèle until 1860. Crown Prince Ludwig of Bavaria, a passionate fan of Rome, came here incognito every year. When they learned he had been made king, his compatriots

Naples and Palermo

In Naples, where coffee became popular only in the 1800s, poet Giacomo Leopardi (1798–1837) sipped his incredibly sweet coffee and wrote his poetry in the Caffè Pinto. In Palermo in the mid-1950s Giuseppe di Lampedusa went every morning to the Caffè Mazzara on the Via Generale Magliocco or to the Caffè Caflisch on the Viale della Libertà to work on his famous novel *The Leopard*.

OPPOSITE: Many musicians are represented in the commemorative wall plaques of the Caffè Greco. Wagner, Mendelssohn, Liszt, and Toscanini were patrons, and their former presence brought future generations of composers and musicians here, including American musical polymath Leonard Bernstein.

ABOVE: A series of rooms with gilded mirrors, portraits on oil, and velvet-upholstered chairs around marble tables, where one sits amid more than two centuries of music and literary figures. The café's present appearance was created around 1860, though it was founded in the 1740s.

Cafés in Literature and the Arts

A Very Selective List

Literature

Joseph Addison's *The Spectator*, nos. 403 and 481 (1711), 568 (1914), contains humorous descriptions of coffee-houses, as do the essays by his friend and contemporary **Richard Steele** in *Tatler*, beginning with the first on 12 April 1709.

Spain's Nobel Prize-winning novelist **Camilo José Cela** set his 1953 novella *Café de Artistas* in a refuge from the suffocating Franco years in Madrid. His great novel *La Colmena* ('The Hive') revolves around a café, a microcosm of Madrid society.

Chapter 132 of *Hopscotch* (1966) by Argentina's **Julio Cortázar** relates his café experiences in Europe.

Slavenka Drakulic's *Café Europa: Life After Communism* (1996) is a political and social memoir of Central Europe.

Ernest Hemingway's short story 'A Clean Well-Lighted Place' is set in a Spanish café; *The Sun Also Rises* (1926) touches on many Paris cafés.

'Coffee', a poem by **Guillaume Massieu**, Professor of Greek at the Collège de France in the 18th century, was originally in Latin (it appears in translation in Aytoun Ellis's *The Penny Universities* (1956).

Carson McCullers' novel *The Ballad of the Sad Café* (1943) was adapted as a drama by **Edward Albee.**

Anna Segher's novel *Transit* (1942) portrays the café life of Marseilles during the flight from Europe at the outbreak of the Second World War.

Johan August Strindberg's novel *The Red Room* (1879) uses this café meeting place for his satire of Swedish society.

Jonathan Swift's letters are full of references to coffee.

The 1946 biography of Balzac by the Austrian **Stefan Zweig** chronicles Balzac's importation and use of coffee, and his growing caffeine addiction, which hastened his death of heart disease and coffee poisoning.

Drama

Carlo Goldoni's 1750 drama *Bottega di Caffè* was set in Venice.

Henry Fielding scored a success with his play *The Coffee-House Politician* in 1730.

Richard Foreman's Surrealist play *Café Amérique* was written in 1980.

Leandro Fernández de Moratín's *Comédia nueva o El café* (1792) is an Enlightenment drama set in Madrid.

Music

Johann Sebastian Bach's *The Coffee Cantata*, a 1732 one-act cantata, was composed in Leipzig and based on the satiric 'Coffee Cantata' by Henrici Picander.

Ludwig van Beethoven played the première of his B-flat trio in 1814 at the first Prater coffee-house in Vienna, in his last public appearance as a piano virtuoso.

Giacomo Puccini's opera *La Bohème* (1896) was based on **Henri Murger**'s novel *Scènes de la Vie de Bohème*, featuring the Parisian Café Momus.

Igor Stravinsky's opera *The Rake's Progress* (1951) was inspired by **Hogarth**'s engravings by that title. Highwaymen frequent coffee-houses during the day and lose fortunes in the gaming room.

Popular songs relating to coffee include 'You're the cream in my coffee' (**Ruth Etting**), 'Let's have another cup of coffee' (**Irving Berlin**), 'One more cup of coffee' (**Bob Dylan**), 'I love coffee, I love tea, I love the java jive and it loves me'

(**Mills Brothers**), 'Black coffee, love's a hand-me-down brew' (**Peggy Lee**).

Visual Art

Le Déjeuner, by French Rococo painter **François Boucher** (1744), shows representative scenes of coffee-drinking among the bourgeoisie in their private circle – a subject relatively rare before 1800.

Rosalba Carriera's *The Turk with Coffee Cup* (1739) is a pastel of a coffee-drinker in Turkish costume, now in the Staatliche Kunstsammlugen, Gemäldegalerie Alte Meister, Dresden.

Edgar Degas' *Café-concert* (1876–7) and *L'Absinthe* (1876) are set in Paris cafés and hang in the Museé D'Orsay.

Salvador Dalí made an Indian ink drawing of Federico García Lorca in the Café de Oriente, Madrid, in 1924.

Gustave Doré's wood engraving *London* (1872) depicts a coffee-house in the working-class district of Whitechapel.

Charles Ginner's *Café Royal* (1911) is in London's Tate Gallery.

Hans Grundig's *Hungermarsch*, set outside the Café Republik, was painted in 1932 and hangs in Dresden's Gemäldegalerie Neue Meister.

In **Renato Guttuso**'s *Caffè Greco* (1976) he includes images of himself, Apollinaire, Picasso, Duchamp and Gide. This group painting set in the Greco hangs in the Ludwig Collection, Aachen.

William Hogarth's copperplate engravings include scenes in White's coffee-house, in the cycle *The Rake's Progress* (folio 6, 1735) and Tom King's coffee-house, in the series *The Four Times of the Day* (folio 1, 1738).

Jürg Immendorf's 19-part cycle of paintings entitled *Café Deutschland* (1977–8) uses café interiors for political and social commentary, Aachen, Neue Galerie.

Edouard Manet celebrates the social life of cafés in his paintings, including *Interior of a Café* (1880), the *Café Concert* (1879), and *Corner of the Café Concert* (1878).

Adolph Menzel painted *Weekday in Paris* (1869) portraying the café as an oasis amid the chaotic metropolis (Dusseldorf).

Johann Samuel Mock's *At Coffee Drinking* represents early 18th century Baroque sensuality, Warsaw, Poland.

Edvard Munch's painting *Henrik Ibsen at the Grand Café* (1898) hangs in Oslo.

In the Coffee Kitchen by **Michael Neder**, painted about 1863, hangs in Vienna's Kunsthistorisches Museum.

In his painting of a Dutch coffee-house about 1650, **Adriaen von Ostade** created one of the first known paintings of a coffee-house.

Picasso painted ten versions of his *Lonely Woman in Café*, beginning in 1901.

In the Café by **Auguste Renoir** was painted in 1877.

The American **Isaac Soyer**'s 'Cafeteria' (1930) hangs in the Brooks Museum of Art, Memphis, Tennessee.

Henri Toulouse-Lautrec's *Star* (1899) presents an English woman in the French concert-café Star in Le Havre.

Vincent van Gogh's *Night Café* (1888) portrayed a place where 'one can go to ruin, go insane, or commit some crime'.

The façade of the Café des Deux Mondes in Paris is featured in a painting by **Tamas Zanco**.

Cinema

Queen of Hearts (1989) features an Italian family setting up a café in London's East End.

Jim Jarmusch's **Coffee and Cigarettes** (2003) focuses on little sketches of people meeting over coffee and the resulting dialogue.

British directors favour scenes shot in cafés: Ken Loach's **Poor Cow** (1967, a café on Fulham Road); David Lean's **Brief Encounter** (1945), Mike Leigh's **Secrets and Lies** (1996), and Peter Howitt's **Sliding Doors** (1998, which uses many shots of the old Regents café on Edgware Road).

Cafés are film backdrops featured in **Café Electric** (Austrian silent film, 1927), **Café Europa** (1960, with Elvis Presley), and Woody Allen's **Melinda, Melinda** (2005).

Watermarks (2004), an Israeli film about an Austrian *hakoa* (Jewish woman's swimming team), includes their final reunion in Vienna's Central Café.

Steve Martin's **LA Story** (1991) contains a memorable scene of contemporary complicated coffee ordering.

Contact Details

PARIS

Café de la Paix
12 boulevard des Capucines
place de l'Opéra
75009 Paris, France
Tel.: +33 (0) 1 40 07 36 36

Le Fouquet's
99 avenue des Champs-
Elysées
75008 Paris, France
Tel.: +33 (0) 1 47 23 50 00

La Closerie des Lilas
171 boulevard du
Montparnasse
75006 Paris, France
Tel.: +33 (0) 1 40 51 34 50

Café du Dôme
108 boulevard du
Montparnasse
75014 Paris, France
Tel.: +33 (0) 1 43 35 25 81

La Coupole
102 boulevard du
Montparnasse
75014 Paris, France
Tel.: +33 (0) 1 43 20 14 20

Le Sélect
99 boulevard du
Montparnasse
75006 Paris, France
Tel.: +33 (0) 1 45 48 38 24

Le Procope
13 rue de l'Ancienne-Comédie
75006 Paris, France
Tel.: +33 (0) 1 40 46 79 00
www.procope.com

Les Deux-Magots
6 place Saint-Germain-des-Prés
75006 Paris, France
Tel.: +33 (0) 1 45 48 55 25
www.lesdeuxmagots.fr

Café de Flore
172 boulevard Saint-Germain
75006 Paris, France
Tel.: +33 (0) 1 45 48 55 26
www.cafe-de-flore.com

Brasserie Lipp
151 boulevard Saint-Germain
75006 Paris, France
Tel.: +33 (0) 1 45 48 72 93
www.brasserie-lipp.fr

ZURICH

Café Odeon
Limmatquai 2
8024 Zurich, Switzerland
Tel.: +41 1 251 1650

SALZBURG

Café Tomaselli
Alter Markt 9
5020 Salzburg, Austria
Tel.: +43 662 844 4880
www.tomaselli.at

VIENNA

Café Central
Palais Ferstel
Herrengasse 14 (corner
Herrengasse/Strauchgasse)
1010 Vienna, Austria
Tel.: +43 1 533 37 64 24
www.palaisevents.at

Café Griensteidl
Michaelerplatz 2
1010 Vienna, Austria
Tel.: +43 1 535 26 92

Café Landtmann
Dr Karl Lueger-Ring 4
1010 Vienna, Austria
Tel.: +43 1 532 06 21
www.landtmann.at

PRAGUE

Café Slavia
Národní trida. 1/1012
Prague 1, Czech Republic
Tel.: +42 0 224 239 604
www.cafeslavia.cz

Montmartre
Retezová 7
Prague 1, Czech Republic
Tel.: +42 0 222 221 244

Café Europa
Hotel Europa
Václavské námésti 25
(Wenceslas Square)

Prague 1, Czech Republic
Tel.: +42 0 224 215 387
www.evropahotel.cz

BUDAPEST

Café Gerbeaud
Vörösmarty tér 7
1051 Budapest, Hungary
Tel.: +36-1 429 9000
www.gerbeaud.hu

Central Kávéház
V. Károlyi Mihály ut. 9
Budapest, Hungary
Tel.: +36-1 266 2110
www.centralkavehaz.hu

BUCHAREST

Café Capsa
Calea Victoriei 36
Bucharest, Romania
Tel.: +40 21 313 40 38
www.capsa.ro

MOSCOW

Central House of Writers
Bolshaya Nikitskaya Ul. 53
Moscow, Russia
Tel.: +7 095 291 6316

ST PETERSBURG

Literaturnoe Kafe (Literary
Café)
Nevsky Prospect 18
St Petersburg, Russia
Tel.: +7 812 312 6057

Brodiachaia Sobaka (Stray Dog)
Isskustv Square 5
St Petersburg, Russia
Tel.: +7 812 303 88 21

OSLO
Grand Café
Hotel Grand
Karl Johans Gate 31
0159 Oslo, Norway
Tel.: +47 22 42 93 90

COPENHAGEN
Café à Porta
Kongens Nytorv 17
1050 Copenhagen, Denmark
Tel.: +45 33 11 05 00
www.cafeaporta.dk

BERLIN
Wintergarten Café
Literaturhaus
Fasanenstrasse 23
10719 Berlin, Germany
Tel. +49 0 30 887286 0
www.literaturhaus-berlin.de

LEIPZIG
Kaffeebaum
Kleine Fleischergasse 4
04109 Leipzig, Germany
Tel. +49 0 178/8 59 21 99

MUNICH
Café Luitpold
Briennerstrasse 11
80331 Munich, Germany
Tel. +49 0 89 292 865

AMSTERDAM
Café Américain
Hotel American
Leidsekade 97
Amsterdam,
The Netherlands
Tel.: +31 20 556 3000
www.amsterdamamerican.com

LONDON
Café Royal
68 Regent Street
London, UK
Tel.: + 44 (0)20 7437 9090
www.caferoyal.co.uk

Kettners
29 Romilly Street
Soho
London, UK
Tel.: +44 (0)20 7734 6112

LISBON
Café A Brasileira
Rua Garret 120–122
Chiado
Lisbon, Portugal
Tel.: +351 21 346 95 41

MADRID
Café Comercial
Glorieta de Bilbao 7
28004 Madrid, Spain
Tel.: +34 91 5215655

Café de Oriente
Plaza de Oriente 2
28013 Madrid, Spain
Tel.: +34 91 541 3974

Café Gijon
Paseo de Recoletos 21
28004 Madrid, Spain
Tel.: +34 91 521 5425

BARCELONA
Café Els Quatre Gats [Four Cats Café]
Montsio 3 bis
Barcelona, Spain
Tel.: +34 93 302 4140
www.4gats.com

Café de l'Òpera
La Rambla 74
08010 Barcelona, Spain
Tel.: +34 93 317 7585
www.cafeoperabcn.com

PADUA
Caffè Pedrocchi
Via VIII Febbraio 15
35122 Padua, Italy
Tel.: +39 049 8764674
www.caffepedrocchi.it

VENICE
Caffè Florian
Piazza San Marco 56–59
30124 Venice, Italy
Tel.: +39 041 5205641
www.caffeflorian.com

Caffè Quadri
Piazza San Marco 120–124
30124 Venice, Italy
Tel. +39 041 5289299 / 5222105
www.quadrivenice.com

FLORENCE
Giubbe Rosse
Piazza della Repubblica 13/14r
50123 Florence, Italy
Tel.: +39 055 212280
www.giubberosse.it

ROME
Caffè Greco
Via Condotti 86
Rome, Italy
Tel.: +39 06 679 1700

Bibliography

Angeli, Diego. *Le Cronache des Caffè Greco*. Rome: Fratelli Palombi Editore, 1987.

Boissel, Pascal. *Café de la Paix: 1862 à nos jours, 120 ans de vie parisienne*. Paris: Anwile, 1980.

Bradshaw, Steve. *Café Society: Bohemian Life from Swift to Bob Dylan*. London: Weidenfeld & Nicolson, 1978.

'Coffee: In Search of Great Grounds'. *Consumer Reports*, December 2004, 47–52.

Deghy, Guy and Keith Waterhouse. *Café Royal, 90 Years of Bohemia*. London: Hutchinson, 1955.

Dicum, Gregory and Nina Luttinger. *The Coffee Book: Anatomy of an Industry from Crop to the Last Drop*. New York: New Press, 1999.

Diwo, Jean. *Chez Lipp*. Paris: Denoël, 1981.

Eckardt, Wolf von and Sander L. Gilman. *Bertolt Brecht's Berlin: A Scrapbook of the Twenties*. New York: Doubleday, 1975.

Ellis, Aytoun. *The Penny Universities: A History of the Coffee-Houses*. London: Secker & Warburg, 1956.

Ellis, Markman. *The Coffee House: A Cultural History*. London: Weidenfeld & Nicolson, 2004.

Falqui, Enrico, ed. *Caffè letterari*. 2 vols. Rome: Canesi Editure, 1962.

Fargue, Léon-Paul. *Le Piéton de Paris*. Paris: Gallimard, 1993.

Fitch, Noel Riley. *Literary Cafes of Paris*. Montgomery, AL: River City Press, 1989. (Publ. in German as *Die literarischen Cafés von Paris*, Zurich, Arche, 1993).

—. *Walks in Hemingway's Paris: A Guide to Paris for the Literary Traveler*. New York: St Martin's, 1990.

Frewin, Leslie, ed. *The Café Royal Story: A Living Legend*. Foreword by Graham Greene. London: Hutchinson Benham, 1963.

—, ed. *Parnassus Near Piccadilly: An Anthology*. The Café Royal Centenary Book. London: Leslie Frewin, 1965.

Gómez-Santos, Marino. *Crónica del Café Gijón*. Madrid: Biblioteca Nueva, 1955.

Haine, W. Scott. *World of the Paris Café: Sociability among the French Working Class, 1789–1914*. Baltimore, MD: Johns Hopkins University Press, 1996.

Hattox, Ralph S. *Coffee and Coffeehouses: The Origins of a Social Beverage in the Medieval Near East*. Seattle: Univerity of Washington Press, 1985.

Hattox, Ralph S., intr. and ed. *Coffee: A Bibliography. A Guide to Literature on Coffee*. 2 vols. London: Hunersdorff, 2002.

Heise, Ulla. *Coffee and Coffee-Houses*. West Chester, PA: Schiffer, 1987. (publ. In German as *Kaffee und Kaffeehause: eine Kulturgeschichte*. Leipzig: Edition Leipzig, 1987).

Junger, Wolfgang. *Herr Ober, ein' Kaffee!* Munich: Wilhelm Goldmann, 1955.

Lemaire, Gérard-Georges. *Les Cafés littéraires*. Paris: Henri Veyrier, 1987.

—. *Cafés d'artistes à Paris . . . hier et aujourd'hui*. Paris: Éditions Plum, 1998.

Neumann, Petra, ed. *Wien und seine Kaffeehäuser: Ein literarischer Streifzug durch die berühmtesten Cafés der Donaumetropole*. Munich: Wilhelm Heyne, 1997.

Oldenburg, Ray. *The Great Good Place: Cafés, Coffee Shops, Bookstores, Bars, Hair Salons and Other Hangouts at the Heart of a Community*. New York: Marlowe, 1999.

Possamai, Paulo. *Café Pedrocchi*. Milan: Skira, 2000.

Pendergrast, Mark. *Uncommon Grounds: The History of Coffee and How It Transformed Our World*. New York: Basic Books, 1999.

Planiol, Françoise. *La Coupole: 60 ans de Montparnasse*. Paris: Denoel, 1986.

Reid, T. R. 'What's the Buzz?' *National Geographic*, January 2005, 2–33.

Robinson, Edward. *The Early English Coffee House: with an Account of the First Use of Coffee*. Christchurch, Surrey: Dolphin Press, 1972 (first publ. 1893).

Rossner, Michael, ed. *Literarische Kaffeehäuser: Kaffeehausliteraten*. Vienna: Böhlau, 1999.

Schorske, Carl E. *Fin-de-Siècle Vienna: Politics and Culture*. New York: Knopf, 1980.

Seigel, Jerrold. *Bohemian Paris: Culture, Politics, and the Boundaries of Bourgeois Life, 1830–1930*. New York: Viking, 1986.

Shattuck, Roger. *The Banquet Years: Culture, Politics, and the Boundaries of Bourgeois Life, 1830–1930*. New York: Viking, 1986.

Szentes, Éva and Emil Hargittay. *Literarische Kaffhäuser in Budapest*. Kiadó: Universitas Kiadó, 1997.

Ukers, William Harrison. *All About Coffee*, 2nd edn. New York: The Tea & Coffee Trade Journal Co., 1935.

Vogel, Walter. *Das Café: Von Reichtum Europäischer Kaffeehauskultur*. Vienna: Christian Brandstatter, 2001.

Index

Acknowledgements

My primary debt of gratitude is to Albert Sonnenfeld, who willingly submitted to requests for translations of documents from many European languages and who has for years shared his love and understanding of Europe with me. He accompanied me to most of the cafés pictured in this book. Translations are his, though any errors are my responsibility.

The bulk of my library research was conducted in the happy confines of the British Library, to which I owe my gratitude.

I am grateful to the countless friends, and friends of friends in Europe, who offered additional personal experience and expertise. Many of them read relevant portions of the manuscript. Their lengthy on-line correspondence was invaluable. Alphabetically by the country of their expertise, they are Kimberly Sparks and Andrew Sorokowski (*Austria*); James Ragan (*Czech Republic*); Hans Hertel, Inge Sloth Jacobsen and Thomas Kruse (*Denmark*); W. Scott Haine, David Burke, Jill and Stuart Griffith, James Rentschler and Alexander Lobrano (*France*); Wolfgang Körner, Kimberly Sparks, Geoffrey Giles, Stanley Corngold and Andrea Frisch (*Germany*); Sandra MacDonald (*Great Britain*); Andrew Sorokowski, Elizabeth Zach and Robin Marshall (*Hungary*); Francesca Italiano, Margaret Rosenthal, David Finkbeiner and Andrew Sorokowski (*Italy*); Dine van der Bank, Peter L. Geschiere and Henk van der Liet (*The Netherlands*); Scott Givet, Lars Rotterud and Jorunn Hareide (*Norway*); Bernard and Basia Behrens, Stoddard Martin and Anna Milewicz (*Poland*); Maria Berza (Vice-President of Romania's Pro Patrimonio Foundation), Val Stoicescu and Leslie Hawke (*Romania*); Ellendea Proffer Teasley, Darra Goldstein, Tanya Nikolskaya and Mary Duncan (*Russia*); Gailyn Fitch Shube, Kathy McConnell, Harvey L. Sharrer, Suzanne Jill Levine and Peter Bush (*Spain and Portugal*); Robbie Wallin (*Sweden*); Susan B Langenkamp and Paul Montgomery (*Switzerland*).

My debt to the published work of coffee and coffee-house historians like Ulla Heise, Gérard-Georges Lemaire, Enrico Falqui, Ralph S. Hattox and W. Scott Haine is enormous. I have been scavenging on the shores of their years of research.

In addition to those mentioned above, I wish to thank my agent, Kate Jones, at International Creative Management in London, and to my editors at New Holland Publishers, Kate Michell and Julie Delf.

Picture Credits